SCREENPLAY

WRITING

STEP-BY-STEP

3 Manuscripts in 1 Book, Including:

How to Write a Screenplay,

Outlining and Story Structure

Sandy Marsh

More by Sandy Marsh

Discover all books from the Writing Best Seller Series by Sandy Marsh at:

bit.ly/sandy-marsh

Book 1: *How to Write a Novel*

Book 2: *Outlining*

Book 3: *Story Structure*

Book 4: *Plotting*

Book 5: *Character Development*

Book 6: *How to Write a Screenplay*

Themed book bundles available at discounted prices:

bit.ly/sandy-marsh

Table of Contents

BOOK 1: HOW TO WRITE A SCREENPLAY 5

BOOK 2: OUTLINING... 70

BOOK 3: STORY STRUCTURE.. 141

HOW TO WRITE A SCREENPLAY

STEP-BY-STEP

ESSENTIAL SCREENPLAY FORMAT, SCRIPTWRITER AND MODERN SCREENPLAY WRITING TRICKS ANY WRITER CAN LEARN

SANDY MARSH

BOOK 1: HOW TO WRITE A SCREENPLAY

STEP-BY-STEP

Essential Screenplay Format, Scriptwriter and Modern Screenplay Writing Tricks Any Writer Can Learn

Sandy Marsh

reparation, damages, or monetary loss due to the information herein, either directly or indirectly.

Respective authors own all copyrights not held by the publisher.

The information herein is offered for informational purposes solely and is universal as so. The presentation of the information is without a contract or any type of guarantee assurance.

The trademarks that are used are without any consent, and the publication of the trademark is without permission or backing by the trademark owner. All trademarks and brands within this book are for clarifying purposes only and are the owned by the owners themselves, not affiliated with this document.

Table of Contents

Introduction.. **10**

Chapter 1: What is a Screenplay?............................... **11**

Physical format 12

Screenplay formats 13

Feature film.. 14

Chapter 2: Television Screenwriting Considerations............ **23**

Drama.. 24

Sitcoms.. 29

Additional Tips to Keep In Mind................................. 33

Chapter 3: How to Create Characters......................... **35**

#5 – Think like an actor 47

What else can we do?... 49

Chapter 4: Creating a Rough Draft **50**

Develop the story idea: 51

Create the pitch: 51

Give it structure: 52

Build a full story: 52

Create a beat sheet: 53

Write the script (finally): 53

NEXT STEPS: 54

Chapter 5: Editing a Screenplay **55**

Chapter 6: Tips for Success **61**

Conclusion **68**

Introduction

I want to thank you and congratulate you for purchasing the book *"How to Write a Screenplay: Step-by-Step | Essential Screenplay Format, Scriptwriter and Modern Screenplay Writing Tricks Any Writer Can Learn"*.

In this book, you will find all of the information you need to begin writing a screenplay, the details on the specifics of the most common types of screenplays, tips on creating believable characters in your screenplays, how to create a first draft and get to work on editing and tips that have worked for the experts.

You will need the information in this book if you want to create a successful script that will catch the eye of producers to get it to the big screen.

To not develop your ability to write a properly formatted screenplay would be Hollywood murder to your career. Style is everything, and this book covers that.

It's time for you to create an amazing screenplay.

Chapter 1: What is a Screenplay?

A screenplay (also known as a script) is a written output made for a television show, a movie, a video, or a game. When it is written for television, it is also called as teleplay.

Screenplay consists of action and dialogue. Action is where a character is noted to do an action, and a dialogue is where the character is speaking. These two components make up around ninety percent of a screenplay.

What sets a screenplay apart from a stageplay are the use of sluglines. This designates where the scene takes place, and what time of day it is, along with the weather that is occurring at the time. These descriptions are important so that the director can make sure that the scenes are set up properly.

Physical format

Screenplays are printed very specifically. They are also all put together specifically as well. This makes it easier for a producer to get through a bunch at one time. They are generally bound with a cardboard cover and a back page to protect the script when it is handled. Oftentimes, the first copy of the script is the only copy. While it is backed up, it takes a lot of paper to print a script most times, so it is important to save where you can.

In America, the script is usually printed single-spaced on letter size paper. It is printed using 12 point courier font. When it is bound, it is bound using a three-hole punch and held together with two brads. One at the top and one at the bottom. This makes it easier to flip through the script quickly.

Reading copies, those which are distributed, are often printed double-sided to reduce paper waste. This is because there are often more copies that will need to be printed later on, and scripts already take so much paper to print anyway, that finding ways to cut down is a must.

Scripts can often be delivered electronically, but many companies require that a certain amount of copies be handed to the company, or at least mailed if travel is not possible.

Screenplay formats

Screenplays come with a certain set of standards that must be met. These standards are ones that help keep everything uniform and allow for easy reading. They form a sort of blueprint for movies and other screenplays. This also allows a company to distinguish those who take things seriously, from those who have a more laissez-faire attitude. There are software packages out there that can help assist with the formatting of screenplays. This makes it easier to ensure that you will have a professional looking piece to show prospective producers. SmartKey, the first screenwriting software, sent codes to existing word processors. However, the ones today have their own macro entities.

Feature film

If you intend to get a motion picture on the big screen, there are a lot of stipulations for how you have to write your screenplay. The headings, formatting, and spacing all have to meet a specific set of guidelines. While the guidelines may vary from country to country, they are all pretty similar in the fact that they have to be uniform. This is because the rate of transfer from page to screen remains around one minute. This gives a rough estimate of how long the piece will run when taken to the big screen. However, some things often get cut, so it is a very rough estimate.

Nevertheless, if you ever want anybody to not only read what you have written, but to truly take it seriously, you will need to stick to the rules in order to ensure that they have as few obstacles between them and getting to the heart of your story. In general, you can think of the concept of screenplay formatting as mainly an aesthetic choice to ensure that every page of your screenplay is as clear and legible as possible. Each script you turn in should always be written in 12-point, Courier font. This goes for movies or television.

The Slug: Luckily, the Hollywood script format is simple once you learn the basics. Every screenplay is divided into different scenes, each of which represents a different location that the story is viewed from. When a new location is introduced in a screenplay, it needs to be described in a specific way so that the person reading it can automatically picture three key pieces of information. They will need to know whether the scene is taking place inside or outside, the time of day it is and the actual location. Together, these three things form what is known as the slug.

Each scene introduction is going to be written so that it appears on a single line, which will include the location details as well as relevant information about the time of day. The majority of slugs will start with either EXT. or INT., meaning exterior or interior respectively. In general, a slug with start with EXT. or INT. and end with either NIGHT OR DAY unless the specific time of day is crucial to the scene. The only time this will not be the case is during parts of the script where the action is repeatedly cutting between two places or is moving through a number of locations, following a character who starts out from a location that has already been defined. For example: EXT. CAVE – DAY

If you have already introduced the cave in the previous example, then you could simplify by writing BACK TO CAVE.

If a character is moving throughout multiple locations inside a predefined location, such as a house, you can write the intervening slugs as KITCHEN or BEDROOM to maintain the flow of the story while still providing the reader with the details they need.

While not required, the slug often also includes the indicator SUPER which is followed by identifying information and indicates what would be superimposed on the screen for example SUPER: 10 years earlier.

If you are writing a conversation between two individuals who are not speaking to one another directly, you can use the indicator INTERCUT BETWEEN after both of the settings have been determined with a standard slug.

The shot: While the shot will also appear in capital letters with a similar type of formatting, it serves a different function when compared to a slug and shot not be confused with it.

As an example: ANGLE ON JACK, C.U. ON GUN. When writing your screenplay, you will use this technique to draw specific attention to an element of the action. It is typically followed by its own description, almost written as an aside, that is always ended with the indicator BACK TO SCENE before the action from the main scene resumes.

Action elements: An action element is going to come directly after the slug and is preceded by a blank line that runs the length of the page. The action element is responsible for setting the scene, literally, as it describes the setting. In it you will introduce what your characters are doing in the scene that will ideally naturally set the scene for what is going to come next. Any action written in this section should be written in real time, which means you are going to want to write as crisply and cleanly as possible in an effort to convey exactly what the audience will see on screen.

When you write your action elements, it is important to leave out as many extraneous details as possible as this makes the script easier to shoot as fewer unique props will be required. The only time you are going to want to go over the top with atmospheric descriptions is when the atmosphere is crucial to what is taking place on screen. For example, if you picture your favorite horror movie, you can bet that the scene that introduced the main location contain an action element with descriptive text.

However, if you are writing scenes that include lots of tense, back and forth dialogue, or action, then you are going to want to do your best to ensure descriptions are kept to an overall minimum. This will help to create an overall feeling of watching the scene play out in real time which naturally makes your script feel as though it could easily be adapted to the big screen.

In order to write action that plays on the page, the easiest thing to do is picture yourself having coffee with a friend and discussing something interesting you saw on your way to the café. This way you will be sure that you cut out all the filler and only focus on the parts that really matter. During these scenes, you are going to want to keep your paragraphs short, no more than five lines in a paragraph, no matter what. Be sure to capitalize any sound effects that are used. Between each paragraph you are going to want to leave two blank lines. By splitting up your descriptions and your action, you are adding an overall visual emphasis to your story, making it feel more like a movie throughout.

When introducing characters, capitalize the entire name, you are also going to want to include a specific gender as well as age. This information is not only going to be crucial when it comes to understanding what is going on in the story, but when it comes to things like budgeting and casting as well. Make sure you don't go so far as to describe specific hairstyles and clothing, except in situations where it is crucial to the plot. You are also going to want to avoid using parenthesis to indicate action when introducing a character. This means no: BOB (cracks a beer).

When describing movement, you are going to never want to use the word camera. Instead, replace it with the word we. This means no: the camera follows, instead it would be: we follow…

Setting up dialogue: The name of the character who is speaking is going to appear in all caps, tabbed in to almost the center of the page and then directly followed by relevant dialogue. The name of the person speaking can either be the name of the character (BOB) or a description if the person isn't known (MAN IN BLACK). Occupations are also acceptable if they are easily identifiable by the average person. If a character is going to play more than an incidental role in the story they should have a name. Be consistent when you refer to a named character, this means no calling BOB by his name in once scene and then by his last name in the next.

Writing Dialogue: The dialogue itself is going to appear located between the left margin, which is where the slug and the action are written and the margin where the character name is written. Writing good dialogue is certainly an art form all to itself, and most new screenwriters make the mistake of over-writing their dialogue.

The end result of this, in most cases is going to be dialogue that comes off more like a play than a movie, which tends to make scenes seem slower than they might otherwise be. It is important to try and keep your dialogue informal, while at the same time not stuffing it full of as much slang as you can manage. If it is important to the story that you character have a regional dialect, you can mention it when you describe them initially, but do not write out their lines in a regional dialect, unless it is a single line written in such a way to indicate emphasis.

When writing dialogue, it is important to make an effort to reflect the personality of each character in the things that they say, while also walking a fine line of not overdoing it. This will make it easier for the reader to picture the conversation as if it were actually happening, as opposed to two characters in a book, spouting soliloquies at one another. This also relates to the way in which key information is relied by the characters in the scenes. You should aim to express inner feelings in a subtle manner, without resorting to on the nose writing where each character simply says what they are thinking or feeling. Your overall goal should be to make the reader, and thus ultimately the audience, feel as though they are a fly on the wall for a real conversation.

Keep in mind that during almost all conversations, the primary players are rarely going to come right out and say whatever it is they mean. Instead, the conversation is going to have subtext. This means you are going to want to leave out bits and pieces of what exactly is going on and allow the audience the opportunity to figure it out on their own. Not only will this make the scene feel more natural, it will be more interesting to watch (or read) as well. For example, in the movie Jerry Maguire, the character of Jerry Maguire uses the phrase "You complete me" to indicate that he is finally ready to express his feelings for the romantic lead. In this instance, the audience knows he means he loves her because earlier in the movie there was a scene of a deaf couple using sign language and a discussion of the sign for love.

While this example is just a little thing, it still makes the audience think, which is a key to keeping them interested in what is taking place in front of them. As such, you are going to want to consider every line of dialogue that you write and the other possible ways that the same intent could be expressed without directly coming right out and saying it.

Parenthetical information: Any parenthetical information that you need to include in your script is going to appear left indented within brackets, underneath the character name. They are used only to express the emotion the character is currently feeling in the moment. For example, (laughing), (angry), or (upset). Any parenthetical information you provide should always be short, descriptive and to the point. As with any ancillary information, they should only be used when they are crucial to the plot.

Transition elements: Certain transitions are going to be optional, these include things like DISSOLVE TO: or CUT TO:. When you use them, they are going to need to be right indented, not flush right, and should only come after a blank line on the page and should always be followed by two blank lines as well. When you come to the end of page without completing a scene, the scene transition should always stay with the shot that was just completed which means you will never start a new page with either DISSOLVE TO: or CUT TO:, those would remain at the bottom of the previous page.

Transitions are primarily used to denote a major shift in time or location, and sometimes, like using MATCH CUT TO:, for effect. You are generally going to want to leave out transition any time you find yourself rapidly cutting between scenes when adding them in will noticeably disrupt the flow of the sequence in question. This is particularly true for chase or montage scenes.

Chapter 2: Television Screenwriting Considerations

The format for television shows differs depending on how long they are supposed to run. Hour-long dramas are written up much like a movie screenplay, however, there are always breaks for act changes. Meanwhile, sitcoms and other, shorter, television shows are written a little differently which means their scripts have different formats to discern what they are supposed to be. The biggest difference between television and movie screenplays is that the level of standardization between genres, or even varying shows is far less well-defined. There are still going to have some hard and fast rules, however, which means the first thing you are going to want to do before you write a spec script is to read several scripts for the show you are going to be writing for so that you get a feel for what makes it unique.

Nevertheless, there are going to be some similarities in this field as well, and it is important that you understand what they are to ensure you get off on the right foot. One thing that is never going to change is the structure of the show in question. A 30-

minute television show is 22 minutes of content and 8 minutes of advertising (in general) and an hourlong show is typically 45 minutes of content and 15 minutes of commercials. The breaks need to be located in the right spots, which means the act breaks, with two or three additional breaks, depending on the network, for hourlong shows.

Drama

When it comes to writing drama, a good rule of thumb is to start every scene already in progress and make sure to move on to the next too early as opposed to too late. Additionally, you are going to want to be extremely selective when it comes to the scenes you do include, each one will need to either develop your characters or advance your plot, there is little room for anything else. The scenes that are going to end on commercial breaks should end on points of high dramatic tension, even if it is not integral to the plot as a whole. Above all you are going to want to keep your focus on showing, rather than telling.

Common types of dramas: There are several major types of dramas that tend to get produced, this is not to say that nothing else is ever going to get on the air, they are just the evergreen types of shows you can always expect to find somewhere on the dial. The first is the procedural, while this was once largely classified to police shows, there are now countless variations on the traditional solve a mystery in an hour formula, and you can find everything from medical to supernatural procedurals on television these days. The next type is the workplace drama, where there is equal focus on the jobs the characters do as well as on their personal lives.

After the success of *Game of Thrones*, the genre drama went from a small niche to big business. These types of shows typically blend fantasy or science fiction with more grounded characters and interpersonal stories. Finally, there are dramas found on premium cable channels, which can fall into any of the categories, but typically deal in much more extreme content matter and also don't need to worry about the traditional act breaks found in non-premium scripts.

Formatting: When it comes to formatting an hourlong script, if you don't have any sample material to look at, you can safely assume that it will be formatted in the same way a feature script would be, more or less, with the biggest difference being the act breaks. Don't forget, the average page of script is assumed to be about one minute, and the average script tends to come in at no more than 60 pages.

The first page, the cover page, that you provide should include the name of the show above the title of the episode above the writer's name. The next page will be the title name and it should include the same information as the cover page as well as your contact information printed below it.

The average episode is broken up into a teaser, which sets the stage for the episode and is what the viewer will see before the title sequence. The rest of the script will then be broken into four acts. Again, this is only an estimate as there are numerous shows that alter this format in one way or another, the best choice is always going to be tracking down a sample script from the show in question if you hope to be taken seriously.

Each act is going to be given a numerical designation and center at the top of the page that starts the act. Broadly speaking, both Act One and Act 1 are acceptable, just ensure that you are consistent throughout. Likewise, the end of each act should by bookended by End Act _. This should be two lines below the final line of text from the act, bolded and centered. FADE or CUT may be used to end a scene, but this is not required. A simple scene slug will do instead. Each new act should then start fresh at the top of a new page.

The average page breakdown per section works out as follows

Teaser: Between two and four pages

Act one: Between 14 and 15 pages

Act two: Between 14 and 15 pages

Act three: Between 14 and 15 pages

Act four: Between 14 and 15 pages

Tag: Between one and two pages

Total: Between 59 and 66 pages

Narrative structure: Broadly speaking, you are going to want to follow a standard three act structure for your script, the first act should set up the goal for the episode and the end of the first act will generally end with them failing to reach some sort of instant gratification. The second act will further complicate whatever it is that the main character is trying to do, while simultaneously raising the stakes. The end of this act will find the character at their lowest point for the entire episode.

Act three typically begins with something that renews the character's resolve and pushes them to get right to the point where they are going to attempt to overcome their obstacle. Finally, act four resolves everything, though the amount to which this is the case is going to be determined by whether or not the episodes are designed for standalone or serialized viewing.

As a general rule, you can expect the average modern series to include the main plot as well as two subplots that all take place at the same time. The main story is the A plot, the B plot is then the more involved of the two subplots while the C plot, also known as the runner, is typically limited to character building moments. These typically occur about three times throughout the episode. If your subplots are going to be referencing specific details from other plotlines of the television show in question, you will need to indicate where in the series continuity it takes place on the title page.

Sitcoms

The first thing you need to understand about writing situation comedies, is that you already need to be adept at telling jokes in order to succeed in the medium. Specifically, you need to concern yourself with timing as if a joke is executed poorly, especially on the page without a comedic actor to save it, it will fall flat every time.

Multicamera: When considering writing a sitcom script, the first thing you will need to consider is if the show you are considering writing a script for is filmed in the multicamera or single camera mindset. In general, you can expect a multicamera shows to have two acts while single camera shows will more often have three.

The general format for a multicamera show is as follows:

FADE IN: this should always be written in capital letters and underlined.

SCENE the scene should be numbered, capitalized and underlined with two spaces above and below it.

Slug the slug should always be underlined .

(Character list) the character list should be written directly underneath the slug and is used to tell the reader which characters are going to be in the scene. It should be encapsulated inside a parenthesis.

DESCRIPTIONS AND ACTIONS both required actions and relevant descriptions are always capitalized, don't forget to keep these to only plot specific requirements.

CHARACTER INTROS this should always be written in capital letters and underlined.

CAMERA INSTRUCTIONS, SPECIAL EFFFECTS AND SOUND EFFECTS this should always be written in capital letters and underlined.

CHARACTER NAMES AND DIALOUGE these should always be written in capital letters and double spaced.

(PERSONAL DIRECTION) this will appear within lines of dialogue, in all capital letters and enclosed in a parenthesis.

The first page after the cover and title page of average sitcom script will start with the name of the show written in capital letters, exactly six lines down from the top of the page and surrounded by quotation marks. Six lines below this you will want to center ACT ONE followed by A on the next line, which indicates the scene, also centered. 8 lines underneath this you will then write FADE IN: so that it aligns with a 1.4-inch margin. This should be followed by the list of characters that is going to appear in the scene. Each page should be numbered and also include the letter corresponding to the scene in question.

The second scene, and each additional scene will then start on a new page. 21 lines down from the top of the page you will put the scene designation, centered. Six lines below that you will then write the slug. Each act will also begin on a new page. When you are writing dialogue, you are going to want to make it double spaced to ensure it is easy to read. When you write stage direction, ensure you do so in all capital letters in order to more easily distinguish them from the dialogue. Each page should contain plenty of white space to ensure actors have space to write their own notes. In general, the following page breakdown should apply.

Teaser: Between one and two pages

Act one: Between 13 and 20 pages, depending on if the story has two or three acts

Act two: Between 13 and 20 pages, depending on if the story has two or three acts

Act three: Between 0 and 13 pages, depending on if the story has two or three acts

Tag: Between one and three pages

Total: Between 40 and 48 pages

Single camera: Single camera shows are typically going to be formatted more like dramas, though again, specific shows may vary. Even if they have commercial breaks, they may not have a traditional three act structure, especially if the entire season is serialized. When writing dialogue, as well as stage direction, you are going to want to make sure that both are single-spaced. Additionally, each character should have their name written in all capital letters the first time they are introduced onscreen. These scripts are typically the tightest of the three, rarely coming in at more than 32 pages in length.

Additional Tips to Keep In Mind

When writing for a sitcom, above all else you need to nail the tone as well as the voice of each character on the show you are writing a script for. The people who will be reading spec scripts know their shows inside and out and they will respond better to those they can tell know it just as well.

Your spec script should be thought of as your portfolio, resume and calling card all in one. As such, you better make sure it is great if you ever hope to get your foot in the door. In addition to being a tight, well-written story, your script needs to be completely free of all errors, if grammar isn't your strong suit, get someone else to edit your script for you. A lack of concern over the little things won't reflect well overall and could easily be the deciding factor between you and another aspiring screenwriter.

In general, you are going to want to stay away from writing a pilot before you have even landed a job in the industry as pilots from unknowns are rarely picked up. With that being said, however, if you have a great idea for a show, write the pilot episode and then write two or three more. By this point your characters will be more well-established and you can show the reader what your average episode is going to be like. This is crucial as the early episodes of many shows are spent establishing character relationships and interactions, leaving less time for traditional activities and jokes and leading to scripts that seem limp.

Avoid using parentheticals whenever possible. Only leave them in if they clearly enhance the dialogue in a specific way. One of the only acceptable times is when the parenthetical will explain body language that will indicate that the character is saying one thing while clearly meaning something else. Likewise, you are going to want to avoid unnecessary explanations, if you can't make the scene work without explaining it, you should cut it, period. Finally, avoid adding scenes just to fill space, if you can fill out a full-length script with useful content it's time to go back to the drawing board.

Chapter 3: How to Create Characters

When it comes to writing a compelling screenplay, the first thing you that is likely going to come to you is going to be the basic outline of the plot. In order to ensure that this basic idea matures organically into a fully fleshed-out screenplay, the first thing you are going to want to do is more fully consider the characters that are going to be going with you on the adventure you are creating. You will find that getting to know your characters more intimately will make the process of actually connecting the dots on the story much more manageable.

You are not just going to want to only focus on creating a protagonist, you are going to want to consider who are going to be the main characters of your story, both protagonists and antagonists, and write character biographies as well. In fact, this is encouraged, especially if you are writing a feature length screenplay. You want a solid backstory and a solid foundation for writing your character into your story. This is a great way to create a very strong character that will draw the audience's attention until the very end.

Always remember the Theory of Illumination. This theory states that every character reflects on your main character. Their relationships, and their development, eventually lead them to your main character. While giving every character a fully-developed backstory on screen is not recommended, knowing the details of a character's life will make them easier to write for in addition to making them seem more well-rounded as a whole.

This means that you aren't going to want to flesh out all of your character bios in a single evening, you need to spend some time to really think each of your characters through. Take a few days where you spend a few hours to think about your characters, this time should be spent without distractions. No phones, no TV, no music, just you and your thoughts, because you want your character to be authentic, not a copy of a distraction that sticks in your mind. You want a truly original person, not a second-rate copy of someone else's character.

Then, you just start writing. Write anything that you feel is relevant to your character's development. Just let your character grow, and pretty much create themselves, with only the manipulation of the outline you have decided on. This is called free association. Free associating is where you let the words take you wherever, and you merely go along for the ride. This allows you to ensure that your character is not too stiff. You want your character to be real, not forced.

This is not say that everything you write during this period is going to be usable, and indeed much of it may be garbage. However, if you can successfully manage to channel your character for this process you never know what useful information you may end up discovering.

You want to follow every major aspect of your character, true, but you cannot neglect the small things that add up to make your character truly who they are. Remember, people are not made up of only the defining moments in their lives, they are also made up of all of the little, seemingly insignificant moments inbetween. You could possibly do a portion where you outline what their day looks like from the time they wake up, to the time they go to sleep. This will help you better establish the type of person your character will be as well.

If you find an area in your character's life, and you are not sure exactly which way to proceed, let the cards fall where they may. If you are still unsure, do a little research, and go from there. You want to know everything about your character, but you can also be surprised where the words take you. Remember, if you don't like what you come up with you can always scrap it later. When writing your script you should only be focused on creating the best story possible, not with how long the process takes you.

Write! Do not worry about if other people will love it, because if you do not, then no one will. You have to first and foremost be able to stand behind your screenplay one hundred percent. Otherwise, it will not be taken seriously. As the quality of your overall screenplay is going to be dependent on the strength of your characters, it equally stands to reason that you need to love them first, before you worry about anything else.

It is important to create dynamic characters and to keep yourself in line with how you want your screenplay to go. The character has to fall in line with what you want to achieve, and yet they also have to bring a certain element to the table as well. They have to create a little bit of chaos, while also maintaining the peace so to speak.

Imagine you are walking a tightrope. You have to have precision balance. That is what making a character is like. You have to have some flaws as no one wants to root for a character that is perfect. However, too many flaws will make your character seem like a mess, and unless your character is actually a mess, you want them to be relatable. So, you have to walk that tightrope between peace and chaos. This is harder than most people think. As it becomes too easy to make a character extremely flawed, or completely perfect. It becomes too easy to fall to one side or the other, and you have to stay in the middle. It is okay to teeter a few times, but you have to pull your balance back up and continue on.

If you are not able to do so, you will find that the whole story veers out of control, and that can make your screenplay less than desirable. This is what you want to avoid for a plethora of reasons, but the first being that you

Here are my top 5 tips for writing stronger characters into your screenplay:

Make your character likable early on: You have to make your character someone that the audience wants to spend at least ninety minutes with. This means you have to make them likable from the get-go. Even if you think the character is interesting, if they are not very positive, or they are annoying, the audience will lose interest before you get to the good parts of the character.

You want the audience to be able to identify with the character because that is what draws their interest in. The main character should be written as the protagonist, this way the main person is not a self-serving, negative drawback to the screenplay, unless the entire purpose of the screenplay is to chronicle their downfall or their redemption. In general, however, people want to see the negative characters portrayed as the antagonist. This way there is some balance between good and bad though, typically, good will win out in the end.

Your character does not have to be perfect, they just have to have some redeeming qualities. These qualities will help your character reach out to the audience in a way that keeps them interested. You can do this by making the dialogue witty and conversational. You can make them do a kind act in the beginning, such as saving a cat from a tree. In fact, there is an entire screenwriting book, entitled *Save the Cat* for just that reason. Regardless of the setup you choose, you just have to make sure that you set the tone for a likable character early on in the story. This is important, because if you do not, you may find that you lose your audience's interest before even grabbing a hold of it properly.

If you have a character that maybe does not have the best qualities, then it is important to include other, worse, characters to make him seem better in comparison. For example, if you have a character that may be in prison, you want to make him better than the other prisoners. Your character does not have to be a saint, just better than the others, and more relatable than a villain. They have to have a sense of purpose about them, to attract the audience to the plot line, and help them retain their interest until the very end. A complex character cannot get lost in his flaws.

Build realistic & detailed characters: While the character is who your person is, characterization is what they are. One is the true deep soul of the character, the other is the shallower, facade that they present to the rest of the world. For example, you could have a lonely woman who just wants someone to love as a character, but her characterization could be a CEO of a company who acts like she does not need anything from anyone. This is characterization. Sometimes the two are similar, and sometimes they are polar opposites. Like a hard, edgy teen is truly a softy on the inside. These contrasts, when revealed, make for a more detailed, believable characters, and a better storyline. People love to be surprised and love finding out more about the characters in a story. So, you have to make sure that you detail their characterization precisely. You want to make sure that you put

some emphasis on who they are, but also what they are as well –
the inside and the outside.

Writing strong characterization is important on so many
levels. First off, a realistically depicted character will add a lot of
realism to your piece. I cannot count how many times I've seen
the same generic antagonist in a film that had zero original
characterization, which ultimately completely diminished their
importance in the film. But even outside of just adding realism to
the characters, it can also help you as a writer to tell your story
more intuitively and dramatically.

Just like you want to write a character biography, you also
want to create characterization sheets. These help you discern
what your character will be like throughout most of the
screenplay. You can do this quickly, through another round of
free association. Give your character choices, as if they were
living, breathing, individuals. It is important for you to be free
flowing with your characters so that they feel authentic and
realistic. If you try to force your character to completely match
someone who inspires you, the character will feel forced. Let the
character speak to you. Which, coincidentally, brings us directly
up to the next tip.

Let your character make the decisions for you: Many writers feel that their screenplay has to be completely mapped out before they even begin writing, and while it is important for you to make sure that you have the structure outlined, it is equally important to let your characters breathe, otherwise the setting will feel fake and forced, which is the opposite of what you want.

Rather than forcing your character into a box that you have neatly outlined before you have even touched the first sentence, you should let your character make their own decisions. This may sound silly because you are the writer, but the truth is, once you have spent enough time with your characters this will seem much more reasonable. Once you have spent enough time chronicling their likes and dislikes, you will find that you will be able to easily picture what they would do when confronted with a specific decision. You want them to come alive and come off the page, which means you have to let the characters take control sometimes. This allows the scene to feel more realistic, and give it more depth.

While your character may be an extension of yourself, they are also a separate entity from you as well and should be treated as such. With that being said, however, if you give a character a trait that you share with them, then it becomes much easier to anticipate how they would act in a given situation as you can use your own experiences as a point of reference.

If you have already created a character biography and a characterization sheet, then this should be an easy thing to do. You should know your character inside out, and as your character grows, how they will make their way through the story should become clear. So, while you might have thought the character could go one way, you may be surprised when you get to that point, and find that another solution suddenly makes more sense.

Likewise, you are going to want your characters to grow organically which means letting them change as the story dictates, as opposed to forcing them to remain in a predetermined box. Not only will this do a disservice to the character overall, it is unsatisfying for an audience to leave a character exactly where they started, either mentally, emotionally or physically, unless that fact is central to the overall plot. You want them to be like real people, because they will be portrayed by real people, and your target audience will be real people, so you have to make sure that your character has depth.

Approach the early drafts with an open mind, and that will help you build an organic, relatable character. Even if it means you have to change a lot because one choice changes everything.

You will find that the more you let your character choose, the more realistic the story will feel, and the more interest the story will garner. This is what you are looking for because you want the character to draw the audience in. It is important that you write some serious choices in as well, as a screenplay without real consequences is likely lacking in dramatic tension as well.

Give your character compelling dialogue: Dialogue was touched on earlier, but it is important enough to warrant further consideration. All of your characters need to have a strong dialogue. This will establish who they are within their first few lines. Even if they do not have a lot of lines, the ones that they have should be solid, and discerning.

So much can be conveyed by the simple use of dialogue. Accent can determine where the character is from. Their sentence structure can determine how educated they are. The tone of voice can determine if they are introverted or extroverted. All of this and more can be shown just by how the character's lines are written.

Something as simple as a scene where a character is running errands, and talking to the people they meet can tell a lot about the character. This may seem odd, but it is true because they are showing a piece of themselves in their everyday life.

Even though the narrative films are fiction, people want them to seem as realistic as they possibly can. This is because people like what they can relate to. They want to be able to feel a connection to a character, even if it is an animated character. Dialogue is a great way to do that.

Compelling dialogue is not always a lot of dialogue. You could have a character that speaks very little, and yet they could be a very dynamic character. How you set up their dialogue really sets the tone for how they are portrayed. You have to make sure that no matter how many lines of dialogue a character has, they are set up to portray a depth to that character.

Something that you want to stay away from is one-dimensional dialogue. This is where all of your characters speak the same. Even if they are all from the same area and same family, every person speaks differently. While similar characters may have similar dialogue, they should also have their own unique characteristics in their dialogue. This will help you discern the different people when the storyline starts speeding up. If you have all the same dialogue, the characters will blend into one another.

#5 – Think like an actor and give your character a point of view

One of the most important things to think about is the character's point of view. As the writer, you see everything, but the main character does not. You have to make sure that you are writing with the character's point of view to ensure that confusion does not set in by the character knowing something that would be impossible for them to know. This clutters things up and makes it hard to keep the scenes straight.

If you are laughing at this tip, you need it the most. You cannot just slap a character down all willy-nilly, you have to put some thought into it. You want a character that will be easy to figure out so that the actor can do the character the justice they deserve.

The most important reason to write a strong point of view is that it gives a line for the story to follow. The audience needs to understand where the character stands, and if the character does not have a solid point of view, then this gets harder to do, and it gets frustrating for the audience, the actors, and everyone involved in the creation of the work you have worked so hard on.

Have you ever seen *Forrest Gump?* In the movie, the main character, Forrest Gump, has a very strong point of view. In fact, the entire movie is told from his point of view. You can see where he stands on life, love, and running. This is what you are looking for in a character, even if it is not written in first person point of view.

There are so many screenplays that lack this concept. These are the ones that often get tossed out because no one wants to be confused for ninety minutes. They want to be able to easily follow the character.

Some scenes are drawn out longer than necessary because the character does not have a strong point of view, which causes the scenes to run around in circles. This makes it harder to follow, and more confusing for the audiences that you may have.

A test to see if you are heading in the right direction is to see if you could cut the scene down to no more than two pages. While some scenes need a lot of dialogue, there are still ways to cut it down to make those two pages, and if you cannot do that, then perhaps you have to reevaluate the scene and the character's strength in their point of view. It is best to do this in the editing stages to see what needs to be changed.

What else can we do?

There is no set formula for how to write a character, but if you follow these tips, you will be off to a good start. It is important that you find what works for you because you have to have a solid character for your storyline to move forward.

In fact, all of your characters need to be strong, so that they move the story along smoothly. A bad character is like a speed bump. It interrupts a steady pace and can be frustrating if there is a lot of them.

There are other tips that you can find from other writers as well. Spend some time with your local writer's guild, or go to the library. This will help you immensely to find yourself and find the character you are looking to create. You have to have a solid grasp on your character, for them to flourish.

Go out in the world, and people watch. You can get some ideas for character traits you would like to have in a character. Walmart, the mall, the park. These are all great places to find interesting characters.

Chapter 4: Creating a Rough Draft

Most contracts that you enter into will give you three months maximum from the pitch to come up with a rough draft. Three months may seem like a good amount of time, but it is actually not a lot of time. You have to work swiftly, and efficiently to get your rough draft out in time. Otherwise, you may lose your shot.

Something that helps is to remember that screenplays are time-related. While a novel can be as long or as short as you would like, most feature films run between ninety minutes and two hours. This makes it harder, and easier at the same time. It gives you an idea of how many pages to write but also makes it that much more restrictive to write with a deadline, and a page limit as well. You want to make sure that you streamline the process, to make things go a lot easier.

Getting a good workflow will give you a good storyline. You do not want to seem like you rushed the development. Here are some ideas for a good workflow.

Develop the story idea:

Before you can come up with a story, you must first start with an idea. You cannot just slap words on a page and call it a screenplay. Go somewhere that inspires you, and get an idea for the story from start to finish.

Create the pitch:

Then you have to create the pitch that will give you an idea of how the story will flow. Start with the five finger pitch. This is where you list some major events on one hand. These events once explained should flow nicely. If they do not go do some more thinking. If they do, then you can move on to the two-handed pitch which is just more events that flow smoothly. Once this is complete, you have a solid foundation for your storyline.

Give it structure:

This is like adding the walls to a house. You have to add more turning points, and supporting events. You want to be able to hold the story up, and by giving it structure, then you can have a full blown story coming your way soon.

The importance of structure is that it keeps the entire story from just falling apart at the seams. If you do not have a strong structure of your house, it will fall down. Same with a story.

Build a full story:

Also known as a synopsis, this is where you get all of the major events mapped out. Basically, the synopsis is a one page summary of the entire story. It is the story without all of the minor details and dialogue. Once this is done, you can move onto the next step, which brings you closer to actually writing the rough draft.

Create a beat sheet:

This is a basic outline that will help you keep track of where the story is at, and where it will go next. The outline does not need to be really detailed, it is just a little bullet point list that you can check off as you pass each point in your writing once you finally get to writing your script.

The importance of a beat sheet is to ensure that you are keeping up with the storyline, and moving at the proper pace. Otherwise, you will find that you are stuck, and being stuck can cost you precious time.

Write the script (finally):

Woohoo! It is finally time to get to script writing. You have to make sure that your outline is complete first, and then you can get down to business. There are a lot of software out there that will help you, as they already have the formatting ready for you. Some also have tips and tricks for writing a good script as well. If you are not sure of your abilities, there are software out there that will proofread your script as well for you, though they are a little more costly.

As you are writing, you may find that you need to tweak what you had previously written. Do not go deleting anything yet, instead, create a list of things that need to be fixed, and when you go to edit your rough draft afterward, then you can create an edited rough draft later on. This way you can keep things on track, and get your first rough draft punched out.

Do not delete your original rough draft. It should be kept as your first draft in case you need to go back and reference changes. Once you have edited all of the additional things into your script, you can celebrate.

NEXT STEPS:

The next step is to get your rough draft to the company you have a contract with. They will look it over, and tell you if they like it, and what they feel needs work. Then you can get to editing.

Chapter 5: Editing a Screenplay

Have you ever wondered why a character is rarely seen eating, drinking water, or going to the bathroom unless it has significance to the storyline? The reason these things are rarely portrayed is that this would be too much information, and would drag the story on too long.

In any storytelling form, you have to edit the life of a character in some way. This will keep the storyline moving, and keep it from getting tedious. Bathroom breaks, minor incidences, and repetitive action are generally not important in a storyline, so if you have too much of these, they should be edited out.

Before a screenplay is produced, there are many ways a writer can edit their screenplays. Whether it be through editing and rearranging scenes, juxtaposition, and cutting the fat. All of these are resources that will help the editing process move forward.

Juxtaposition is important to use in any form of art, and screenwriting does not escape its grasp. Just by changing the juxtaposition of scenes, you can give the story an entirely different feel.

This can be used in one scene or two scenes, or depending on how many you need to use it on to help get the point across.

Crosscut and parallel action are two points of juxtaposition that are most commonly used in writing, and they are found to be very effective in creating different tones for different scenes, which is what writers want to achieve.

For instance, a very fun moment cut directly into a boring moment can accentuate that boredom through contrast.

Juxtaposition is a word that is not overlooked in any editing class. It is useful in so many areas, from writing to cinematography, and stage preparation. Prop work as well. The contrast it creates can be useful in setting a tone and creating a mood. This makes it less necessary for words to set the tone, which will leave you more words for important things.

Sometimes, you get so attached to your story that you do not want to cut anything, but the unnecessary parts are important to cut because they just slow the production down. It is important to cut them before they get to production if possible because you do not want to waste more time than you absolutely have to.

Some directors are more spontaneous though. They want you to leave it all in, and they will see how it works as it is being filmed. However, if you cannot get a scene to work when you are writing it, it is still best to leave it out.

However, if you are lower budget, you should make all of the necessary cuts before production, because any delays can cost a lot of money. If you do not have that much money, to begin with, then you will have a hard time recovering.

Removing weaker scenes do not just help production, they help the budget as well. Every page of the script costs money, and if you cut the weaker scenes that wouldn't make the cut anyway, then you save the money it would take to produce them.

Cutting scenes post-production also causes a lot of problems with continuity in a piece as well, because there is not enough time to smooth out the edges.

The continuity of a film is really important. Without that continuity, it will feel like someone gave a twelve-year-old a camera and told them to make a movie.

It is important to take the lighting into consideration as well. Consider how the light will affect the mood. So when editing, you have to pay close attention to the lighting to make sure it stays consistent. Fix it if you need to because the wrong lighting could set the wrong mood, which would shut your whole production down. If you do not want that you will make sure to specify the time of day in every scene.

Not only does the light change, but your character may also change as well. If a lot of time progresses, your character cannot stay the same the entire time. You have to make sure that you have made note of the changes as the film progresses.

The visuals are usually clear-cut, but if scenes need to be cut in post-production, that can disrupt the visuals. If several scenes need cut, then you may find that certain scenes need to be reshot to fix the visuals. This is another reason to focus on editing closely.

When editing, it is important to keep in mind the order of the scenes to ensure that the continuity is there. If something needs to be switched around, make sure to adjust it accordingly, so that the visuals are smooth, and there are no visual speed bumps when you hit production. Because it becomes a lot harder to fix on the spot then, and you want a smooth transition to have a successful film. Visuals are very important, and it is important to remember that.

Another part of editing is to make sure that you note the transitions. Every film has to have transitions between scenes so that they flow smoothly. Otherwise, you would have to add a whole lot more information. These transitions are a lot easier to add in the editing process than the post-production days. So make sure to make a note of the transitions before it becomes harder to add them.

Another reason to make sure everything is solid in editing is that there can be unwanted interpretations if you have to cut scenes in post-production. Doing so between similar scenes can create confusion, and doing so between contrasting scenes can be jarring and dramatic. This can be used to say something if it is intentional. However, if it is not intentional, you risk saying something to the audience that you never meant to say, which can leave them confused.

Also, directors do not like to be told how to do their job, so avoid technical directions in your script. Instead be subtle in telling the director where the camera should be pointed. Instead of saying "Point camera to the west." You could say "The main character looked off into a beautiful sunset, contemplating the meaning of life. Since the sun sets in the west, the camera will point west.

Editing can save you from a lot of issues later on in life and ensures smoother transitions as you head into production. It is important to make sure you edit out all of the kinks to save money when it comes time to shoot the film. Now if only taxes could be edited out of our lives.

Chapter 6: Tips for Success

While there are a wide variety of reasons that you might want to be a screenwriter, if you are hoping to do so in order to adopt a shorter, less stressful, work week you may be extremely disappointed. In fact, successful screenwriters are often extremely disciplined, dedicated individuals who have trained themselves to create something from nothing, day end and day out in order to ensure they always have something productive in the pipeline. While what works out to be an effective process for each writer is going to differ, sometimes dramatically, the most successful all typically have a number of habits in common that make the task before them more manageable. These are outlined here, in hopes that at least a few of them will inspire you to write more successfully in the future.

They have a reason to write: The best screenplays, especially those written by first time screenwriters are written with a specific purpose in mind, by writers with a driving desire to tell a specific story. This doesn't mean that your motivations for telling your story need to be pure as the driven snow, after all, entertaining others is as good of reason as any. The important thing is that you have a reason that is strong enough to drive you to continue trying to tell your story no matter how hard the going is going to get, and it is likely to be quite difficult from time to time.

Regardless of the motives that you have for writing, you need to be passionate about it if you ever hope to find true success. Don't feel ashamed if part of the reason that you want to write a successful screenplay has something to do with egotism, remember, the goal isn't to make yourself want to write a screenplay that will change the world, it is to find what drives you to write, and in this case egotism is as useful of a reason as any. Everyone wants recognition to some degree, and if you want to write for revenge, glory, fame, money, power, or simply to prove that you can, then you can harness that energy and use to make you a better writer, ensuring you actually see the screenplay through in the process.

They demand the best from themselves: When you first start writing your screenplay, it is perfectly acceptable to leave in placeholder scenes and text, from time to time, just to ensure you make it through to the end in one piece. With that being said, it is important to keep in mind that the spec script your produce is going to be the one, and often only, thing that people in the industry look at when they decide if they are going to give you your big break which means that settling for anything less that absolute perfection is akin to throwing away all the time that you ultimately spend on your screenplay.

As such, it is important to never settle with your first draft, your second or even your fourth. You are going to want to go through the entire thing with a fine-tooth comb until the story is as tight and compelling as possible. While this is only going to ever take you so far, it will at least ensure that the screenplay that you send in is the most accurate indication of what you are capable of as possible.

At the same time, you are going to want to make a conscious effort to stop making changes at the point where the work, as presented, speaks for itself as you can always find something to tweak or change. Eventually you are going to need to have the confidence in yourself to put the work out there and, hopefully, start receiving feedback on it. If you don't practice restraint, your screenplay will likely end up feeling overwrought, as you will have overthought whatever spark was there to begin with into oblivion.

They write what they like, and what they know: While anyone can have an idea for any type of story, and that story might be unique, or relatable, enough to resonate with the world at large, you will typically find that it is much easier to write about things that you have first-hand knowledge about and also much easier to keep at it if you like whatever it is that you are writing. Again, it is perfectly acceptable to get into the screenwriting business for its potential for lucrative gains, this in no way means that you can't enjoy the process along the way. What's more, if you find the story in your screenplay exciting, the odds are high that those around you are going to feel the same way.

Likewise, when it comes to writing what you know, this doesn't mean writing a movie about being an accountant for an accounting firm, unless you have an idea that will make the process seem roughly 2,000 percent more exciting than the topic naturally seems to the average person. Rather, adding in touches from your every day life can make certain characters more believable, or giving one of your hobbies to a character can make them seem more three-dimensional. What's more, you never know when something from, even a seemingly boring job, can provide you with the one realistic, but unexpected, fact that you need to tie the whole plot together.

They set goals: If you have never before found yourself sitting in front of a blank screen, with all the freedom in the world in front of you, only to find yourself looking for any excuse to be anywhere else, then the idea of setting writing goals to ensure you actually finish your screenplay may seem unnecessary. The first time you make the decision to bolt rather than face down your writer's block, however, you will realize just how vital setting goals can be. Likewise, if you have never written anything substantial before, then you may find yourself doing all the research you need to complete your screenplay, only to find that you never actually get any closer to generating a truly finished product.

As such, you should start by setting goals for your pre-writing process, including generating characters, a basic plot synopsis, world building elements etc. You should give yourself plenty of time for the more free-form nature of this part of the process, though you should have a firm deadline when you want to begin the actual writing to ensure that fleshing out your characters doesn't end up taking years to finish.

When it comes to writing the first draft, you are going to want to make a concentrated effort to write for at least an hour a day, at least five days a week, and also spend some time on the sixth day coming up with a general idea of where the end of the next week should find you. Writing every day will help to ensure that you don't lose the flow of the story as it can be hard to recapture lost momentum once it has slipped away. While writing for a set period of time is fine, you will find that you will be more productive still if you task yourself with writing a set number of pages each day. This will ensure that you maintain your productivity, rather than just waiting out the clock on days where inspiration takes longer to strike. In addition to page goals, you are going to want to have a general idea of where you want to the story to go next, so you can steer things in that direction.

When it comes to editing, you are going to want to set hourly goals, as it is difficult to say just how much work you will get done per session as it is going to vary so dramatically. When it comes to setting an overall timeline for completion, you are going to want to give yourself enough time to ensure you don't rush, but not so much that you don't feel obligated to make daily progress. When setting these goals, it is important to keep in mind that they are not taking place in a vacuum. Writing for three or four hours every day is an admirable goal, and likely one that is completely unrealistic if you already have a fulltime job. It is important to set goals that are achievable as failing to do so can harm your morale and making finishing your screenplay harder than it already is.

Finally, the overall length of your timeline isn't important, as there is no standard amount of time it should take to create a quality screenplay. The most important thing overall, is that setting a schedule will help you to make finishing your screenplay a priority which means you are going to be far more likely to finish it than you otherwise would. Remember, your screenplay could be your shot at the bigtime, but the only way you will ever know for sure is if you actually finish it.

Conclusion

Hopefully, you learned a lot about writing a screenplay from this book. It was filled with plenty of tips on how to proceed. This is important because you cannot just jump in.

Now, you can go out, and start working on your screenplay. This book can be your guide if you whenever get stuck.

Thank you and good luck!

OUTLINING

STEP-BY-STEP

ESSENTIAL CHAPTER OUTLINE, FICTION AND
NONFICTION OUTLINING TRICKS
ANY WRITER CAN LEARN

SANDY MARSH

BOOK 2: OUTLINING

STEP-BY-STEP

Essential Chapter Outline, Fiction and Nonfiction Outlining Tricks Any Writer Can Learn

Sandy Marsh

reparation, damages, or monetary loss due to the information herein, either directly or indirectly.

Respective authors own all copyrights not held by the publisher.

The information herein is offered for informational purposes solely, and is universal as so. The presentation of the information is without contract or any type of guarantee assurance.

The trademarks that are used are without any consent, and the publication of the trademark is without permission or backing by the trademark owner. All trademarks and brands within this book are for clarifying purposes only and are the owned by the owners themselves, not affiliated with this document.

Table of Contents

Introduction..**76**

Chapter 1: The Basics of Making an Outline.........................**78**

What is an outline? 78

Who uses an outline? 79

The importance of using an outline 80

Outlining for fiction vs. Non-fiction............................ 82

Plot outline vs. synopsis.. 83

Understand the plot of a story................................... 84

Why is it important to understand the plot?.................... 88

Chapter 2: Fiction Outline **89**

Snowball Method... 89

Pure summary 91

Skeletal outline 93

Bullet outline.. 96

Chapter outline 99

Sequence outline 100

Flowchart outline 102

Visual outline 103

Chapter 3: Non-Fiction Outline 105

Pure summary 105

Skeletal outline 107

Bullet outline 108

Chapter outline 110

Research 113

Chapter 4: Best Practices 114

Know your characters 114

Know your story 116

Keep it simple 117

Be flexible 118

Have a clear premise 121

Take a break 123

Choose and organize your ideas 124

Observe proper sequence 125

Focus on the main points 126

It does not have to be perfect 127

Remember that an outline is just a guide 129

Take your time 130

Have your sources ready 131

Ask yourself questions 133

Practice 135

Conclusion **138**

Introduction

Congratulations on purchasing this book and thank you for doing so. The following chapters will teach you all the important things that you need to know about making an outline. Learning to make an effective outline is an invaluable tool as a writer. It can help the writing of your book to flow more smoothly, work out more conveniently and be organized.

Chapter 1 talks about the basics of making an outline. This will give you a good foundation and understanding of what outlining is all about. Chapter 2 discusses how you can make an outline for a fiction book. Chapter 3 teaches how you can make an outline for a non-fiction book. Chapter 4 lays down the best practices that you should observe when making an outline.

Writing a book can be a daunting task. By using an outline, you can make the process of writing a book simpler and easier. The good news is that it is not hard to make an outline as long as you know what you are doing. An outline is an effective tool and is the secret behind an effective book writing. By learning how to make an outline, you are able to cover a significant part of the actual book-making process. Take the outline as a blueprint, the guide, or architecture, of your book.

Chapter 1: The Basics of Making an Outline

What is an outline?

An outline works as a guide when it comes to writing your book. Take note that a book is a big world. Without a good outline, you can easily get lost in the process of writing your book. An outline ensures that you stay within the plot that you want for your book and that every scene works towards building your story.

It is worth noting that an outline only serves as a guide. A writer has the option whether or not to stick to their outline. Still, having an outline is helpful because it will give you a sense of direction. It is also a useful tool to use to ensure proper sequencing of events or scenes in your book.

There are different ways to make an outline. This book will teach you notable and effective methods to outline a book, both for a fiction book and a non-fiction book. Indeed, learning how to make an outline is an invaluable tool that should be in the arsenal of every writer.

It can be said that an outline is the book itself but in a very simplified version. It can also deal with the technical aspects of the book, such as the timing as to when and how a certain characters or ideas will be presented. Consider the outline as the blueprint or the foundational architecture of your book.

Who uses an outline?

Almost all professional writers use an outline. Some go as far as saying that all writers *should* use an outline. The use of an outline does not just refer to books, but even in other forms of writing. In fact, it is not uncommon even for article writers to write an outline for their more complicated articles. An outline ensures that the focus of your writing and the proper flow remain concentrated. So, if making an outline is really this important, are there known authors who apply them? The answer is yes. Here are some examples to name a few: The author of *Harry Potter*, JK Rowling, James Salter, Paulo Coelho, Sylvia Plath, Jennifer

Egan, William Faulkner, and many other popular writers have admitted the use of outlines in the creation of their works. As you can see, using an outline is considered such an essential skill and tool of a writer that even well-known authors use it regularly.

Should you use an outline? Well, just because you are a writer does not necessarily mean that you are required to make an outline before writing your book. So, whether you want to use an outline or not is a matter of personal preference. Still, it is worth noting that many writers have realized the benefits of using an outline.

The importance of using an outline

It is worth noting that there are some authors who do not use an outline when they write a book. Instead, they simply allow the natural current of the work to drive them to somewhere, hoping that it would be worth telling. However, the truth is that many of these of authors have outlined the book in their mind, so somehow, they still have that sense of direction. Of course, there are also those writers who completely have no idea of what they are writing and just see where the writing goes. After all, when it comes to writing, especially when it comes to writing fiction, there are no hard and fast rules to limit a writer. You are free to write your book in whatever way you want just as you are also free not to write a book. However, if you want to be sure of your sense of direction and not waste your time writing on so many pages only to realize that they do not make sense, then you should use an outline. An outline is also easy to make, yet it will assure you that your book has a good flow and direction.

Now, there are those who say that using an outline will only limit your imagination, so they do not want to use an outline when they write a book. They do not want the outline to "cage" the expression and flow of their ideas. However, this is not the correct way to view an outline. Take note that as a writer, an outline is still just an outline. You are not in any way compelled to follow your outline all of the time. For example, let us say while you are writing the setting of the story as stated in your outline you realize that a different place would be more suitable, then you are free to use that place instead of what is in your outline. Of course, the same principle applies to the other parts of the book.

Again, an outline is a helpful guide that will ensure to give you a sense of direction; it should not, in any way, be seen as an obstacle or a cage that limits your imagination. You are strongly encouraged to stretch and explore the beauty of your mind. In fact, even an outline comes from the creative mind of a writer. The outline can be thought of as the skeleton of the book that you hang the actual story on.

Outlining for fiction vs. Non-fiction

Outlining works for any kind of book, whether fiction or non-fiction. However, making an outline for a fiction book is not the same when you make an outline for a nonfiction book and vice versa. This is because of the inherent differences between the two genres. In a fiction book, for example, a novel, you will need to spend more time outlining the plot of the story and the sequencing of the events.

You should be able to present your characters effectively and build up the story. In the case of a non-fiction book, there is usually no need to build up any story. Instead, you should focus on presenting the right information. Of course, the proper sequence should also be observed. In a fiction book, the outline will be mostly composed of the setting, the characters, and the different events that take place in the story. In a non-fiction book, the outline will be divided into main topics and subtopics regarding technical subjects.

Although there are differences between making an outline for fiction and nonfiction, the use and purpose of an outline still remain the same, and that is to make writing the book easier and more organized.

Plot outline vs. synopsis

Many people use these two terms interchangeably. However, it is worth noting that they are not the same. Take note that when you create a plot outline before even start writing a book you then use the outline as your guide as you write, so that you will be guided on how the story should flow. Writers who use plot outlines are usually called "plotters" since they plot the whole story before they even write it down. This is a good way to avoid writing too many drafts with rejected scenes and pages.

A synopsis is usually written after the completion of the book. It refers to the summary of your story or novel. The synopsis is usually a part of a proposal letter that a writer sends to a potential publisher.

A synopsis can be as short as a single page or even up to five pages. A plot outline can also take a single page but can be longer than five pages. It depends on how much you work on your outline. If you add in more details, then it will be able to guide you once you proceed to write your story. In addition to the story, a plot outline can include a detailed character story and other events.

Some writers already know their story before they even write it. So, if you can come up with the synopsis first, then you can use that as a guide to make a more detailed outline.

Understand the plot of a story

If you are into fiction writing, then it is important for you to know the plot of a story. What is a plot? It is what draws readers into the story. It refers to the arrangement of the story elements. There are generally five parts of a plot: the beginning or exposition, rising action, climax, falling action, and denouement or ending. Let us take a look at them one by one.

Exposition

The exposition is the beginning of a story. Hence, this is the part where you present your characters. Take note that the characters are not the only ones that develop your story. You also need to pay attention to the place, as well as the time. Unfortunately, some people forget about the element of time. Do not forget that Paris today was much different a hundred years ago. It is also important to keep the exposition as interesting as possible. You need to make it grab the interest of your readers; otherwise, they might stop reading your book before they even find out the about good and exciting parts.

Rising action

This is where you build up your story. This is usually where a problem is presented, and the characters take steps to face or solve the problem. This is also what prepares the most exciting part of the story, the climax. The rising action is where you build up the anxiety and the expectations. This is also the part where you start to tug at the hearts and emotions of your readers. The more attached the readers are to the characters, the more powerful the climax and the overall story will be. It is important that a writer build up the story effectively; otherwise, the story may become boring to the reader.

Climax

This is known as the turning point and the most exciting part of the story. This is where the emotions are at their peak. Nothing is ever the same as this point. This is where real and solid changes take place. Usually, immediately right after the climax, everything takes a downhill, relaxes, and prepares for the ending.

Falling action

This is the part where the story falls and takes a downhill, which leads to the ending of the story. Here, the story usually comes together, and the missing pieces are finally resolved. This is also where you reward your audience. Take note that your readers normally associate themselves with the protagonist in the story, so you use this part show them how the protagonist is rewarded for all of his or her labor. This is also a good part to impress on the readers the moral of your story if any.

Denouement

This is the ending of the story. Here, the loose ends are tied, and the questions are finally answered. Of course, it can be a happy ending or a sad ending. A story can even have an open ending where there is technically no end and you leave to the reader the final conclusion of the story.

Why is it important to understand the plot?

As a writer, it is important for you to understand the plot. When you make an outline, you actually work on the plot of your story, such as how are you going to begin the story, how do you present your characters, the time and place, etc. before then you moving on to the rising action, then the climax, and so on. As you can see, it is important to have a good understanding of the plot because the story revolves around the plot that you set. There are also writers who make an outline by simply filling in the parts of the plot with details.

Chapter 2: Fiction Outline

Snowball Method

The snowball method is one of the most popular techniques for making an outline. Just like a rolling snowball that gets bigger and bigger as it rolls downhill, the snowball method starts with just a simple topic, idea, or a scene. It will then be continuously developed, and it will branch out to more ideas, more scenes, and other parts of the story.

For example, let's start with the simple idea of a man who falls in love with a woman. Let this idea be the very center of the snowball. This will also be the main theme of the story. We now branch out a little and give them each a name. Let us say that the name of the man is Jack and the name of the woman is Mina. So now we have the protagonists of the story, as well as the central theme of love. Of course, Jack cannot just fall in love with Mina out of nowhere. So, we add another part to our snowball: let us say for example that Mina is in need of money. She then applies for a job at a nearby restaurant which happens to be owned by Jack. Let us say that Mina is able to get the job as a waitress, and she then works as a waitress gets to meet other people who work at the restaurant. Again, this is another part of the snowball.

When working as a waitress, one day, Mina encounters a very rude customer. Again, we let the snowball turn, and we simply continue to add more information or details. For example, let us say that the rude customer is the one who complains and calls for the manager of the restaurant who happens to be Jack as well, the owner. Jack then is able to put the situation under control. That evening, Jack calls Mina to his office for a meeting. Mina is anxious about it because she does not want to lose her job. Again, we simply let the snowball turn and gather more details. Contrary to what she has expected, once she is already in the office, Jack appears to be very polite and even apologizes for what happened that day.

This is simply how the snowball method works. Simply put, you just have to keep adding more and more details. If you continue to do this, then you will soon come up with a short story, a novelette, or even a novel. From one small snowball, you simply let it roll and roll and gather more ideas and details to turn it into a big snowball, a complete story. Also, do not forget that you are writing an outline and not a story just yet. So, keep it simple and short, but be sure that the main points of the story are there.

Pure summary

As the name implies, a pure summary outline is the kind of outline that is composed of summaries. This is like the short version of your entire book or novel. You simply have to summarize everything, such as chapters, scenes, and others.

The idea behind this method is to write down your whole story from beginning to end, but only write down a compressed version. To do this, just write down the important parts or highlights. You can skip all forms of dialogues and just focus on telling what is happening in the story.

For example, Ana is looking for a job and applies as a journalist. She gets the job and as she works as a journalist, she gets to meet Ryan, a photographer, who happens to work in the same company. Despite their busy schedule, they do their best to make time for each other. One day, Ana is in an accident and

Ryan does his best to serve her. To save her life, he has to go into an ancient forest and get a golden apple from a mysterious tree. He ventures into the forest and meets Galdorf, a friendly elf. Galdorf helps him find the mysterious tree and battle the Dark Witch of the forest. By doing so, he frees the imprisoned elves and also saves Ana from dying. They live happily ever after.

As you can see, every part of the story is compressed but it is complete. All that you need to do is to fill in the details. The good thing here is that you are already given a clear roadmap or guideline as to how your story will flow from start to finish. In fact, by using this approach, you will already be able to imagine your story as a whole, and all that you need to do is to write down the details to make the story come alive.

The pure summary is one of the best ways to make an outline. Just summarize every chapter or sub-chapter from beginning to end. When done, you will have a complete story. All that you need to do is to clarify every point by adding in more details.

Skeletal outline

You have probably learned this kind of outline in school or for any other academic purposes. The key to this method is to input the core points in the right order that will best present your story. This is an effective way to get a bird's eye view of your story, including its overall structure. Take note that the structure of a book or story is essential. A book that is poorly structured, whether fiction or non-fiction, will most probably have problems with being disorganized and have confusing contents. A skeletal outline will allow you to easily reform your story or book, which will allow you to create the maximum impact out of your story. Let us take a look at a simple example of a skeletal outline:

Exposition

- The setting of the story takes place in a small village called as Sestin.

- The story introduces Adam, who is a farmer.

- The story then introduces Monica, the daughter of a rich businessman

Rising action

- Adam meets Monica as he tends the farm of her father.

- They get to know each other for some days.

- One day, goblins attack the village of Sestin.

- Monica is held hostage by the goblins.

Climax

- Adam fights the goblins and saves Monica.

- The story also reveals that they both share the same mutual feeling for each other.

- It is found that Adam is actually of royal blood and owns a kingdom

Falling action

- The father of Monica allows Adam to marry his daughter

Denouement

- Adam and Monica get married and everyone is happy.

- They all live happily ever after.

Take note that this is just an example of a skeletal outline. It may be shorter or even much longer than this. The important thing is to plot the story and the events properly. It is also worth noting that this kind of outline is not just applicable to fiction writing. You can also use it for non-fiction works. This will be discussed in more detail later in the book.

A good thing about this approach is that it allows you to see the structure of your book more clearly. Usually, a skeletal outline clearly divides the book into parts and is just composed of single lines. When taken together, they all compose a whole story.

Bullet outline

- A bullet outline is one of the most common types of outlining. In fact, this is one that is widely used by people even if they do not read about it. With a bullet outline, you simply have to make notes in bullet form as to what will happen in the story. For example:

- Lisa is an accountant.

- One day, she meets Mr. Gibson, a high-stakes gambler.

- They get to know each other better.

- They fall in love with each other.

- However, Mr. Gibson's gambling addiction starts to become a problem and begins to affect their relationship.

- Lisa tries to help Mr. Gibson and does her best to save their relationship.

- (and so on and so forth)

This is an example of a bullet outline. So, how do you use this outline? It is actually fairly simple. Using the example, at first you expound on the part of the outline that says, "Lisa is an accountant." A good way to do this when you actually write your novel is to describe the nature of Lisa's work. Make it as meaningful and interesting as possible.

If you look at the next part of the sample outline, the next part is "One day, she meets Mr. Gibson, a high-stakes gambler." Of course, you would not have to write this line as is. Rather, just like the first bullet, you make it more details. How did they meet? Perhaps Mr. Gibson starts to have money problems and needs an accountant to save his business. You can explore and expound on this once you actually start to write the book. Take note that this single bullet alone can take a whole chapter. This is just to give you an example of how to use a bullet outline more effectively.

A bullet outline is a very simple yet effective method. Another benefit of using this kind of outline is that it gives you a lot of room to exercise your imagination once you start to write the story. The outline focuses more on the flow of the story instead of what is actually happening in the story.

It is common to use a bullet outline on a per chapter basis. Many writers first prepare an outline in bullet form before they begin writing a chapter. This way, they can be sure that they know the direction of the story. Every bullet point is also usually short, so it would not be hard for you to follow it. Once you have a well-established outline in bullet form, then all you need to do is fill in the details of every bullet point and not worry about the direction that your story will take.

Chapter outline

A chapter outline divides a story into chapters. Every chapter will then have an outline of what is going to happen in that particular chapter. Here is an example:

Chapter 1: The Meeting

Noah calls for all the soldiers to attend the secret meeting.

Every soldier attends the meeting, except for Jason.

Jason, the number one soldier in the world, wakes up in a hospital with amnesia.

Even though Jason is not able to attend the meeting set by Noah, Noah is soon able to follow his tracks and visits him in the hospital.

Noah reminds Jason who he really is.

As you can see from the example, the book will be divided into chapters and every chapter will then be divided into sub-topics or events that take place in the story. A chapter outline is a good method, especially if you are particular with every chapter in your book.

As is usual, only the main points are included. This is to give room for you to exercise your creative imagination when you write the story. The outline is just enough to guide you as to what will happen next and avoid the situation where you get stuck up not knowing how to make the story to flow continuously. A chapter outline is also one that is commonly used by writers.

Sequence outline

A sequence outline puts more focus upon the sequencing of the events in the story. However, it still outlines the important points, so even this method alone would be enough to help you with writing your book. Here is an example of this kind of outline:

1 - Dianne, still a very young child, is baptized as a witch.

2 - Her parents were killed for practicing sorcery.

3 - She soon grows into one of the most powerful witches.

4 - Dianne meets King Gregory, the man who had ordered for her parents to be burned at the stake.

(and so on and so forth)

As you can see, there is a fine outline of the sequence of the events. If you are the type of writer who finds it hard to stick to the flow of your story, then a sequence outline may be the one for you.

Although you can add in as many details as you want, it is important to stick to the sequence; otherwise, a change may have major effects on the story as a whole. Take note that if you mess up with even just one part of the sequence, then you should check how it affects the other parts. Are they still logical enough when taken together? This method is also commonly used by writers. It is also like a bullet form outline but is more particular with the sequence of the events and the flow of the story.

Flowchart outline

This approach makes use of a flowchart. This is similar to a sequence outline but makes use of a chart that is also in proper sequence. Here is a simple example:

Adam works as a painter --> He attends an event for artists --> While at the event, he sees and meets Stella --> He falls in love with her at first sight --> and so on and so forth.

As you can see, the scenes or parts of the chapters are reflected through this flowchart. When you finally start working on the book, then you will add in the details to every point in the chart. A single part of the flowchart can cover a few pages up to a whole chapter, depending on what is happening in your story. So, for example, let us take the first part of the flowchart: Adam works as a painter. When you write this in your book, you can then expound on this topic. You describe the nature of his work and you can also write and show what happens in his life as a painter. As you can see, just these things alone can take many pages, even a whole chapter.

The thing with a flowchart method, just like any other outlining method, is for you to pinpoint the main parts of the story and ensure that you arrange things in the right order. Once everything is set, then you simply have to add the details when you write the book.

Visual outline

If you are fond of drawing, then this style of outlining may be the one for you. When you use a visual outline, all that you need to do is to draw the main events in a story, especially its plot. Take note that instead of writing in words, this approach lies in drawing and making figures. For this, you may want to use a notebook. You can fill each page with a drawing that would illustrate what the scene will be. You then follow it up with another scene on the next page, and so on and so forth.

Even if you cannot draw well, you can still use this approach. After all, just like any other outlines, this is something that you do not need to show to anyone else. An advantage of using drawings instead of words in making an outline is that you will have more room to play with the words, as well as for the exercise of your imagination. This is because every drawing can have diverse meanings and significance. If you want a style of outline that will give you maximum use of your imagination once you begin writing your book, then perhaps using a visual outline is a good idea. However, the drawback is that this kind of outlining may not always work for everyone. In fact, the very reason why you want to make an outline is to have a good sense of direction when you finally write your book. The risk is that you may not be so inspired when you finally write your book that the drawings may start to look boring or empty to you.

Chapter 3: Non-Fiction Outline

Pure summary

Just like for fiction writing, you can also use the pure summary approach for non-fiction book writing. When you use this approach, simply make a summary of the information. This means that you do not have to explain anything. Just make a summary of every chapter in the book. For sub-topics, you can simply write a one or two-sentence summary. Again, this is just a summary, so there is no need for you to expound or explain anything. Still, it is worth noting that when you read a summary, the stories must be coherent and logical enough. In other words, it must still be a complete story with proper flow and structure. However, of course, you do not want for it to too detailed. After all, it is just a summary, which can be a summary per chapter or even per sub-topic in every chapter. The important thing is for the summary to mention the main points of the book. This will also ensure that you will not forget about them.

When you use this method, then it is also important that you pay attention to the sequence of the information. A common rule in non-fiction writing is to start from the basics, and then gradually branch out to more complicated matters on the subject.

In non-fiction, you are not expected to make a well-detailed summary considering that there is a chance that you still need to learn more specific details about the topic in question. Of course, if you know exactly what you are writing about then you may only require a minimum level of research; however, if you are writing something about which you do not have enough knowledge, then there would be little that needs to be summarized. If you want, you can just research and study the subject first before you start to make a pure summary outline. However, do not let the lack of research prevent you from using this approach. After all, you have the convenience of having open books and information both when you make an outline and when you write the book.

Skeletal outline

A skeletal outline is common in non-fiction writing, especially when the book deals with a technical topic. This is because a skeletal outline offers exactly what you would need for non-fiction writing. When you use this approach, you begin with a subtitle, which may be the name of your chapter. You then identify and specify the skeletal outline of the book with the topics and sub-topics that you will discuss in the book. Needless to say, this follows the same format as the one for fiction. However, unlike a fiction book, this does not follow any plot. Rather, it has a more logical flow to it. For example, when you write a book about bitcoin, you should not talk about bitcoin mining right away. Instead, you should start with the basics, such as what bitcoin is, what a cryptocurrency is, and others, and then make your way up from there.

Bullet outline

A bullet outline is excellent when you deal with specifics. For example, when you make an outline of a chapter or sub-chapter in a book. Also, what you can do is to highlight the name of a chapter, and then simply outline in bullet form what you want to talk about for that part of the book. For example, let us say that you want to write a book about the cryptocurrency Bitcoin, here is a sample outline:

Chapter 1: The Basics of Bitcoin

- What is Bitcoin?

- What is cryptocurrency?

- What is a cryptocurrency wallet?

- Who uses bitcoin

- How does a bitcoin transaction work?

- (and others)

As you can see, every point is made clear. All that is left for you to do is add the details. Of course, you can further use the bullet outline like this:

Chapter 1: The Basics of Bitcoin

- What is Bitcoin?

    - a digital money

    - uses cryptography

- What is cryptocurrency?

    - cryptography for secure communication and transaction

- What is a cryptocurrency wallet?

    - a place to store cryptocurrency

    - kinds of cryptocurrency wallets (hot and cold wallets)

- Who uses bitcoin

- anyone with an Internet connection

- How does a bitcoin transaction work?

    - Input

    - Recipient's wallet address

    - Amount

As you can see, this makes it more detailed and it will be easier to fill in the information once you start writing the book. When you write non-fiction, outlining your work is more practical. After all, non-fiction works do not deal so much with one's creative imagination. The important thing is for you to be able to cover the technical details and be able to present them effectively.

Chapter outline

A chapter outline is one of the simplest ways to make an outline for a non-fiction book. Basically, you simply have to write the name of the chapter, and then add in the titles of the sub-topics within a chapter. This is also like a bullet form of outlining but is more general. Of course, you can also make it more specific by further outlining the sub-topics just like in a bullet outline. In fact, both kinds of outline are very similar to each other.

The first step in a chapter outline is to set the titles of the chapters. Again, as a rule in non-fiction, you should start with the basics. The reason is that you must first establish a foundation for your readers before you delve into more complicated matters. A common mistake committed by writers is to assume that the reader already knows and understands the topic. If you come to think of it, this understanding is highly flawed. After all, a reader would not have to waste time reading your book if he is already aware or if he already understands what is written in your book. So, never assume that the reader can easily understand what you write. Instead, have an open mind and consider the reader as someone who knows nothing about your subject. Of course, this is subject to some exceptions, for example, if you target readers are really those who already have an idea of your subject. A good example of this will be the advanced guides or manuals.

Once you have the titles of the different chapter ready, then it is time for you to add in the subtitles that will be placed under each corresponding chapter. You should be careful about the subtitles because they are the ones that will lead the development of the book. Hence, they are the ones that will form the structure of the book. Just stick to the basic rule of starting with the basics and then work your way up, and you will be fine. This is just a matter of presentation. Feel free to try different combinations until you find the one that feels most natural and convenient for a reader.

The number of chapters will depend on the kind of book that you write, as well as the number of words of the entire book. Normally, the longer the book is, the more chapters it will include. When you write your outline, be sure to pay attention to how many chapters your book will have, as well as the number of sub-topics that you will be using. It helps if you have more sub-topics so that you will not run out of things to write about. However, take note that book writing is not about the length but the quality if your book. Hence, it is important that you focus more on the quality of your writing that on the number of chapters or subtitles that your book has.

Research

Although not considered as a complete outlining method, when it comes to non-fiction writing, research is the main tool that you have in your arsenal. Although you are still free to use your imagination, non-fiction writing has certain restraints upon one's writing. The golden rule is that you cannot contradict a fact. Well, except, of course, if you have another set of facts to present that can support your view. Take note that when it comes to non-fiction writing, the facts are your friends. Needless to say, in a non-fiction book, almost everything that you write should be backed up by research or at least verifiable. This is to make your writing more believable and credible.

In non-fiction writing, it does not matter how good your outline is if you do not understand the subject. Hence, make sure that you have all the necessary materials to get to know your subject and do as much research as possible. The more that you know your subject, the easier it will be for you to come up with a good outline, and the easier it will be for you to complete the book.

Chapter 4: Best Practices

Know your characters

When you write a story, especially in fiction writing, it is important for you to know your characters. It is worth noting that an outline is not something that you use to get to know your characters. It is important for you to know the characters first before you make an outline.

Take note that the characters are important as they are the ones that tell and develop the story. If there are not enough characters or if you do not know your characters well enough, then the story will not grow properly. Therefore, is important for you to know and understand who your characters are. In fact, once you know your characters, then telling the story will come naturally as the characters themselves will play out the story. This is the part of writing a story where the writer becomes a mere observer of his characters. You can allow your characters to lead you. This will give you an idea of what the story will be and, so it will be easier for you to make an outline.

If you do not know your characters yet, especially your main characters in the story, then you should give yourself more time to get to know them. You do not necessarily have to know all your characters completely. You will know if you already have sufficient understanding of your characters when the characters themselves are able to lead and create the story for you. Needless to say, every character must have his or her own persona and should act according to that personality.

A suggested way to know your characters is to interview them one by one. This is a common practice used by novel writers. So, how does it work? Just imagine talking to your character. Ask them questions and see and feel how they respond. This may seem strange to some people, but many writers use this approach. They talk to their characters to the point like they feel that they are merely recording (writing) what the characters in the story are telling them. Once characters are given a persona and existence in the story, it will seem that they really have an identity and life of their own. Hence, talk with your characters and ask them questions. Learn from them. This way you will be more able to develop your story.

Know your story

Take note that your plot is like the skeleton of your story. Therefore, when you write a plot it is also important that you already have an idea of what your story is going to be. When you write an outline, it is not important for you to know the minor details and the dialogues of the characters. However, it is important for you to know the main points of your story or the main events that will shape your story. These are the things that will constitute your outline.

The more that you know your story, the easier it will be for you to make an outline of it. After all, making an outline is as simple as recording essential details and skipping dialogues and other things that are considered important to a novel. It is more focused on simply having a worthwhile story instead of discussing all the things that happen in a story.

Now, it is also worth noting that many writers write an outline even without knowing their story. How is this possible? Well, they allow the process of outlining to reveal the story to them. To do this, you just need a basic idea. You write it down as part of an outline, and then simply add more details to it to continue to grow your idea. Since you are just making an outline, it does not have to be too detailed, and you should just focus on the main points that will help develop the story.

Keep it simple

It is important to keep your outline simple. Remember that your outline should not be a cage that will limit your imagination. Rather, it should serve as a guide that will help you come up with a meaningful story. Therefore, keep your outline simple, including only the main and important points that should be in your story.

As a rule, small or minor details should not be placed in an outline, except if they are important to the story. The reason why you do not include everything in your outline is to prevent the outline from limiting you to exercise your imagination as you write your story. Again, an outline should only serve as a guide.

You also do not have to make your outline beautifully worded. Do not forget that the outline is only for your own eyes, so you do not have to spend so much effort in finding the right combination of words. You can save such effort for when you finally write the book. Instead of worrying about the words that you use, focus on the story that you want to tell, as well as the flow of the events and information.

Be flexible

It is worth remembering that an outline only functions as a guide. As such, it is not required for you to always stick to your outline. This is important for you to remember, especially if you suddenly come up with a better idea than the one in your outline while writing the story. This is another reason why you should keep your outline as simple as possible. By keeping it simple and just including the important parts of the story, then you will have more room to exercise your imagination.

It is considered very common for writers to suddenly stray away from their original outline. This is why you should not spend so much time worrying about how your outline is written. After all, it is still just a guide for you; and being the writer, you are free not to follow your outline.

Flexibility is important. Normally, the story only reveals itself fully even to the writer only when you actually pen down the story. This may sometimes come as a surprise, even to the author himself. As you write your book, the more you realize what the story is really all about. Simply put, as you follow your outline, you are also led to discover more about it. Now, from time to time, you may have to change course and take a completely different one than what you have originally outlined. This is normal, but just be sure to take a better path than the previous or current one. Also, if you ever change your course, you may want to stop for a while and reflect on the direction of your new outline.

A normal part of flexibility is to be flexible enough to update your outline. Yes, an outline can undergo so many changes and modifications as you write your book. Take note that you do not need to write new outlines, rather you can just edit your current outline little by little.

A common mistake committed by writers is to change a part in an outline and then allow the new storyline to lead the way without him knowing where it will actually go. Then this happens, then it is as good as writing without an outline. Now, I am not saying that this approach is wrong. Again, there are no hard and fast rules about how to write a book. However, if you are the type who cannot write properly and organize your thoughts without a guide, then what you should do in this case is to update your outline. Yes, updating an outline is something that you should do every time you make even minor changes to your outline. The outline must remain logical and coherent all throughout. This will ensure that your novel or the story itself will also be logical, coherent, and well structured. After all, your very story is just the outline itself, only that it now has more details. For example, if your outline says that Samantha is beautiful, then your story will make descriptions or show certain scenes to show just how beautiful she is. Still, the very essence of the writing can be traced back to your simple outline. Outlining and being flexible go hand in hand. Although there are writers who stick completely to their original outline and do not let anything divert their path (which is not wrong per se), sometimes it is good to be more open and allow changes to take place, especially positive changes.

Have a clear premise

Even before you work on an outline, you should first establish your premise. Ask yourself:

- Who is/are my main character/s in the story?

- Where does the story take place? In what year or time?

- What is the conflict in the story?

- What will be the turning point of my story?

- What message do I want the story to communicate to the readers?

- Who will be the enemies in the story, if any?

Once you have answered all these questions, then it means that you have a good idea of what your story will be. Take note that these are just basic questions. You are free to expound and ask more specific questions. But, these questions will reveal to you the premise of your story or what it is really about. Now, in case you find it hard to answer these simple questions, then it only means that you need to think about your story even more. Do not forget that an outline can only be made if you have a story to tell. Although an outline does not need a complete story, it requires that its essential elements should be present.

When you ask yourself these questions, it is important that you be completely honest with yourself. It is unfortunate that some writers delude themselves and hate saying" I don't know." Take note that this is a normal part of the writing process. The more that you admit to yourself the parts in your story that are still unclear to you, then the more you will understand what your story is really about. After all, the act of writing is still an act of self-discovery. You do not need to have the answers right away. It is normal to accept that you do not know the answers to some questions; the important thing is not to stop to seek for an answer. Of course, to do this, you need to reflect and delve more into your story.

Take a break

Just as you take some breaks to finish writing a book, you should also give yourself time to take a break when you are working on an outline. It is not uncommon for professional writers to spends days just to work on their outline. If you are just starting out to learn how to write and use an outline, then feel free to take as much time as you need. Just do not forget that an outline should make the writing of the book to easier in the long run. Unfortunately, some writers get too caught up writing their outlines that they fail to even start writing the actual book.

You will also be able to think much more clearly and be more creative if you allow your mind to relax. In fact, writers are strongly advised to give themselves a break from time to time even while working on the actual book. It is not uncommon to find writers who go to the beach and spend time on vacation while working on a book. This is because you will be a much more effective writer when you allow yourself to rest. With a fresh and rejuvenated mind, you will be able to use your creative talent more effectively.

Choose and organize your ideas

A book comes from an outline. But, where does an outline come from? Yes − an outline comes from ideas. However, it is worth noting that in the process of writing a book, it is very common to experience being bombarded with lots of ideas. For example, let us take a simple example where you present a protagonist in a story. Let us say that your hero is a man who happens to work in secret service for the government. There are tons of different ideas that you can use to show this. There are also many ways by which the story can go. Does he have super powers? Is he going to die and then resurrect? Or is he just an ordinary person who just happens to be good at what he does or maybe he is not even good at his job and merely relies on luck. The thing is that although outlining is a way to record and organize your ideas, you should also choose the ideas that you will be using in your story.

Now, once you have organized the ideas in your mind, it will then be easy for you to plot your story by making an outline. It is simply hard to make an outline when you know that you yourself do not know your story.

Observe proper sequence

When you write your way outline, it is important for you to pay attention to the proper sequence of the events or information. If it is a fiction book, I then the building and arrangement of the story should be in proper order. If you are writing a non-fiction book, then the information should be in an ordered sequence that will make the information more understandable to your audience. This is important especially if you are writing about a technical topic. For a fiction book, you should build up the story from beginning up to the end. In case of a non-fiction book, then you should share the information by starting from the basic details, and then continue building your way up to more complicated topics or sub-topics in the book.

Making an outline is the best way to set the proper sequencing of events of your story. Unfortunately, some writers still write the bulk of words only to end up with a confusing storyline. By making an outline, you can easily work on the sequence of the events of your story. In fact, you will be able to view and imagine your story completely, and all that will be left for you to do is to add in the details.

If you ever find yourself having a hard time putting things in the right sequence of ideas or events, then it is usually a sign that you should pause for a while and try to understand what is really going on in your story. Sometimes the logical sequence itself will be the one to guide you as to what to write next.

Focus on the main points

Making an outline is simply making a list of the important points of the book in proper order. You should focus on the main points. For a fiction book, the main points will be the beginning of the story, the rising action, climax, falling action, and the denouement. In the case of a non-fiction book, the main points, of course, would relate to the important details regarding your subject.

It is worth noting that some minor details may also be considered a necessary element in the development of a story. In this case, you can include the said minor details in your outline.

But, what are the main points? How do you know if a certain detail should be considered a main point and be included in your outline or not? Well, it depends. If the detail or information is something that is important in building up the story, then it is to be considered a main point and should be included in your outline. However, if it is something that your book or story can do without, then it is just a minor detail. The important thing about making an outline is to give you a good sense of direction. It has to function as a logical road map of your thoughts even if you forget about your story. After all, it is not uncommon for writers to think of an exciting plot only to have it slip away before they are able to get it written down completely. Whenever this happens, a possible wonderful story is lost to the world.

It does not have to be perfect

An outline does not need to be perfect. Keep in mind that it is just a guide. Hence, there is no need to follow it to the letter. Even if you come up with what you believe to be a perfect outline, know that it is still just an outline. As such, you should not allow yourself to be limited by it.

It is also worth noting that no matter how perfect you think your outline is, there is still a chance that it may be revised or modified. This is true, especially in the case of novels. It is not uncommon for writers to start at something specific only to be taken by the story somewhere more beautiful than they had imagined before writing the book. Does this mean that writing an outline is not important? Of course not. An outline assures that you maintain sense and direction in your story. However, it is worth noting that it considered common for writers to make changes to their outline several times as they write the book. Now, you should be careful when you do this. As a general rule, you should not change your original outline. You must stick to it. However, as an exception, you may change your outline if you are able to come up with a better version of the story. It has to make the story more exciting or meaningful for the readers. If not, then you need to stick to your outline. This is the reason why you should not aim to have a perfect outline because such a thing simply does not exist.

Although you do not expect an outline to be perfect, it does not mean that the outline can just contain every thought that you think would be good for your story. An outline must still be carefully written. How can you expect for your outline to guide you if the ideas do not match up well with one another or if the outline itself fails to follow a logical sequence? Hence, it is important that you work on your outline, but do not aim for perfection. Having the right ideas and correct flow would be enough.

Now, just because an outline does not have to be perfect does not mean that you should not give it as much time as it deserves. The outline, after all, serves as the foundation of your book. Therefore, take as much time as you need when making your outline, which leads us to the next topic: time.

Remember that an outline is just a guide

Although an outline can be regarded as important, do not forget the fact that an outline is still just your guide. Therefore, you are free to stick to it while you write the book or totally abandon it halfway. However, this does not mean that an outline is no longer important. But, you need to understand this so that you will not end up like other writers who get too obsessed with their outline.

Remember to see and use your outline as a guide in writing the book. You are always free to change or revise your outline as many times as you want and in any way that you deem best.

Take your time

When making an outline, you should take as much time as you need. Although your outline will not be a part of your book, it is still the foundation of your book. Consider it like a business plan or blueprint of your masterpiece.

Although you can make an outline in as fast as a few minutes, it is not uncommon for professional writers to spend even a week to work on an outline. This is true, especially if you want to create a high-quality book.

You should also learn to organize and manage your time. Unfortunately, there are many writers who commit the mistake of procrastinating. The temptation to procrastinate is something that you should watch out for when you write a book. A good way to avoid procrastination is to set daily objectives. For example, aim to be able to finish 15% of your outline every day. Also, take note that writing an outline is just part of the process. The more important part is for you to write your book, which will take more time and effort than writing an outline.

Have your sources ready

This is true, especially if you work on a non-fiction book. You should have your sources ready. This is because sometimes it is hard to look for your sources during the time of actual writing. A good way to keep your outline more organized is to cite your sources in the outline. One of the main reasons for using an outline is to make the work of writing the book easier for you.

You do not have to cite your sources formally. After all, the outline is your own private document. You do not need to show it to your readers or anyone else. The purpose of having your sources ready and to cite your sources is for you to be ready when you write your book. So that when you write the book, you will know exactly where to look for information as you fill in every major and minor topic in your outline. Even fiction writers can use the same approach. After all, many fiction stories also incorporate real-life events. Take, for example, *Da Vinci Code*, which combines fiction with non-fiction information.

When it comes to writing non-fiction, it is important to take note that you should stick to the facts. If you want to force your creative thought and ideas into the page, then you might want to consider shifting to fiction writing. It is worth noting that readers of non-fiction books read not mainly for entertainment or pleasure, but to get as much as useful information as possible. They do not care about your opinions unless your views have a good basis and foundation. Hence, it is important to identify the kind of genre that you want to write in even before you make an outline. This is because the style of writing and even the expectation of the readers have certain distinctions between fiction and non-fiction writing. As for the sources, be sure to quote from credible sources. If possible, use internationally known and accepted formats like APA or Chicago when citing your sources.

Ask yourself questions

Okay, so now you have a clear idea of how to make an outline. But, how do you know which types to include in your outline? The key is to ask yourself questions, the right questions. For example, when writing fiction, let us say that you have a character named Max. Now, ask yourself, who is Max? Let us say that Max is a poet.

Ask yourself who is Max as a poet? What is he like? Once you are able to answer this then you can have something to place in your outline: Max is a poet who writes for a princess who does not even know that he loves her. Next, ask yourself what happens next. You may come up with the next part of the outline, like: A big event is about to take place and Max and the princess are going to attend the said event. The next step is for you to imagine the event and ask yourself what happens to Max at the event, and so on and so forth. As you can see, by simply asking yourself the right questions, you can develop a story.

How about for non-fiction writing? Well, a similar technique can be used. However, if you are dealing with a technical topic, let us say a book about Blockchain technology, then you should ask a different kind of questions. For example: What is blockchain? What are the types of blockchain? What is the history of blockchain? This continues until you come up with a highly informative book.

It is important to ensure that every part of your outline should help develop or enhance the book. This way you can be sure that your book will be interesting and informative.

Okay, so how do you know the right questions to ask? It is simple. You just have to take the perspective of a reader who does not know your book or subject. Therefore, if it is fiction writing or when you write a novel, if you have a character in mind named Gabriel, then ask: Who is Gabriel? What does he do? Where does he live? All these questions will soon open up a whole new story that is full of meaning and value. Now, in the case of non-fiction writing, again just consider that a reader is a beginner in the subject that you are discussing. Therefore, you should start with the basic details and lay down a good foundation. After which, you can then talk about more complicated topics within your subject matter.

Practice

When it comes to learning how to outline properly and more effectively, nothing beats practice. So, if you want to learn how to make an outline, then just start practicing it. Make an outline for the next books that you write. No matter how much you read about it, it remains true that the only way for you to appreciate and realize just how beneficial making an outline can be.

Learning how to write a good outline is just like learning to write good books. This means that you simply have to practice it by applying it regularly. If you get good at writing outlines, then the task of writing a book becomes simpler and more manageable.

You do not have to learn the different ways to outline a book. After all, when you make an outline, you only need to use one method. If you want, you can combine two methods at once. There is no strict rule as to when a particular method should be used over another. Therefore, feel free to use the one that you are most comfortable with.

For those writers who are against the use of an outline:

Indeed, there are some writers who do not like the idea of using an outline. It is worth noting that this book does not make it a requirement or an obligation of a writer to use an outline, but merely shares how helpful an outline can be in the process of writing a book. Therefore, if you strongly prefer not to use an outline, then you are free to do so. In the world of book writing, whether or not you use an outline does not matter in the end. What matters is the final product, which is the book itself. There are writers who use an outline and know for sure how useful it is, while there are those who simply allow the story to unfold like a surprise. The only disadvantage of not having an outline is that it is common to follow a story only to meet a dead end or you just realize that the story has become dull and boring.

An outline assures that before you even start working and writing your boo, you are assured of a good sense of direction. All you need to do is write, and even if all that you do is to stick to your outline and not change any parts of the story but merely add in the details pursuant to your outline, then you can be sure that you will end up with a good book, provided that you have prepared a good outline.

Once again, it is up to you as a writer whether or not to use an outline. The best way to find out what works for you would be to give it a try. Write a book without an outline and then write one that has a proper outline, and see which writing experience is better for you. In the end, it is not about whether or not you have used an outline, but how much the book has made your soul grow in the process.

Conclusion

Thanks for making it through to the end of this book. We hope it was informative and able to provide you with all of the tools you need to achieve your goals whatever they may be.

The next step is to apply everything that you have learned and start making an outline of your book. Learning how to make an outline is one of the best things that should be in the arsenal of every writer. It is useful and makes the book writing process easy and manageable.

If you are a beginner, you might encounter some difficulties writing an outline for the first time. The key is to not be too strict about it. It is worth noting that the methods revealed in this book are also just guides. You, as the writer, has all the right to make your own modifications. In fact, you may want to develop your own way of making an outline. The important thing is for you to know and understand how to use it to help you in writing a book. Keep in mind that there is really no right and wrong way of making an outline as long as it is able to help you write your book. After all, the very purpose of an outline is to help a writer and make the process of writing a book simpler, easier, and more organized.

When you write a book, it is not uncommon to suddenly feel so lost. Some writers have a story to tell but do not know how to start or how to maintain a smooth flow of the pages. This is why making an outline is important. There is a big universe out there, and you need to place only the right stuff into your book in proper order. Indeed, the task of a writer is not an easy thing. But, if you learn how to use an outline, then you have an invaluable weapon that you can use to make the writing process so much easier.

Good luck!

STORY STRUCTURE

STEP-BY-STEP

ESSENTIAL STORY BUILDING, STORY
DEVELOPMENT AND SUSPENSE WRITING
TRICKS ANY WRITER CAN LEARN

SANDY MARSH

BOOK 3: STORY STRUCTURE

STEP-BY-STEP

Essential Story Building, Story Development and Suspense Writing Tricks Any Writer Can Learn

Sandy Marsh

reparation, damages, or monetary loss due to the information herein, either directly or indirectly.

Respective authors own all copyrights not held by the publisher.

The information herein is offered for informational purposes solely, and is universal as so. The presentation of the information is without contract or any type of guarantee assurance.

The trademarks that are used are without any consent, and the publication of the trademark is without permission or backing by the trademark owner. All trademarks and brands within this book are for clarifying purposes only and are the owned by the owners themselves, not affiliated with this document.

Table of Contents

Introduction... **148**

Chapter 1: Purpose of Story Structure.......................... **150**

What is a Story Structure? 150

Where do Story Structures Come from?...................... 151

Why You Need One.. 152

Chapter 2: The Essentials of Building a Structure.............. **155**

9 Step Process 155

Step One: First Act 156

Step Two: The First Major Plot Point........................... 157

Step Three: First Half of Second Act........................... 158

Step Four: Second Major Plot Point 159

Step Five: Second Half of Second Act 160

Step Six: Third Major Plot Point 160

Step Seven: Third Act.................................... 161

Step Eight: Climax.................................... 162

Step Nine: Resolution 163

Chapter 3: Developing Your Story..................................... 165

Study Existing Plots.................................... 165

Draft Up Your Plot 167

Create a Timeline.................................... 168

Plan Character Development Along the Plot Line....... 169

Change the 5 "W's.................................... 169

Design a Story Board.................................... 171

Consider Subplots 171

Incorporate Driven Elements 172

Question Yourself.................................... 176

Get Feedback 178

Chapter 4: Creating Suspense 180

Understand Your Genre 180

Provide Adequate Viewpoints 182

Put Time on Your Side 183

Keep The Stakes High 184

Don't Be Afraid to Apply Pressure............................... 185

Make Use of Dilemmas 187

Complicate Things.. 188

Avoid Becoming Predictable 189

Develop Your Villain.. 190

Develop Your Hero... 191

Chapter 5: Additional Story Structure Tips 193

Research Different Story Structures 193

Stick to Structures that Are Traditional for Your Genre
.... 195

Structure the Novel to Your Central Theme................. 196

Modify the Template to Suit Your Plot 198

Create the Structure First, Modify it Later 200

Hide the Structure in Your Writing 201

Keep Your Structure Organized and Handy 203

Experiment.. 204

Take Notes 205

Conclusion **208**

Introduction

Thank you and congratulations on purchasing *"Story Structure: Step-by-Step | Essential Story Building, Story Development and Suspense Writing Tricks Any Writer Can Learn"*.

This book was created to help you learn a series of tips and tricks that will help you enrich your story and make it a must-read book for your target audience. By using these techniques and strategies in your own book you will be able to generate a storyline that is rich with suspense, action, and other tools that are important to keep your readers engaged and excited about reading your book.

Each chapter within' this book is dedicated to one element of story structures themselves, ensuring that you are provided with the greatest in-depth detail to ensure that you learn plenty to help you produce a phenomenal story. Before the book ends, you will be provided with tips from top writers and authors that will help you write like the pros.

This book was not designed for any particular experience level when it comes to writing. Instead, it has been populated with tricks that will help any writer from beginner to advanced. If you are someone who typically struggles to write stories but you are looking to get yours heard, you can be certain that you will learn some tips here to help you get on your way towards having your book completed. Likewise, if you have done this before but are looking for a refresher or are otherwise interested in learning more to enrich your story and create an addictive read for your audience, you are certainly going to learn something also.

Please be sure to take your time and work through all of the tips and tricks provided within' this book. While some may not be entirely relevant to the work you are producing, they may provide you with inspiration to move forward in a more powerful way. As well, be sure to keep this book handy for future writing ventures as you never know which part will stand out each time. Finally, remember that writing is an experience that should be enjoyed by both the reader and the author. Be sure that you take the time to make the process enjoyable for yourself so that you can produce your best work. And finally, have fun!

Chapter 1: Purpose of Story Structure

Understanding the purpose of story structure will ensure that you are aware of how it can make (or break) your story, and why it is so crucial that you develop a strong structure within' your own story. Prior to diving into any important tips or strategies, we are going to explore what a story structure is, exactly, and what purpose it serves within' your story.

What is a Story Structure?

In basic form, a story structure is essentially a map that is drawn to take your reader from point a to point b. You want them to start at the beginning of the book and end at the end, only after being taken through an experience which is essentially each "stop" on the map. This map is used to help identify how people solve different problems, as well as to assist in conveying the message that the author is attempting to send from the storytelling process. In essence, the structure of your story is the process where the outline is transformed from being a simple idea to being the bones of your story. It becomes the part that holds the entire story up and gives it a form that is both natural, yet moving.

Where do Story Structures Come from?

Story structure is less of an invention or creation and more of an element of the story that was observed and thus plucked from the process and used as a tool to help generate new stories. For thousands of years, humans have been telling stories to one another whilst using story structure without ever knowing what it actually was. This is the part of the story that was used to draw listeners or readers forward through the story while keeping them actively engaged and wanting to know more. With the use of story structure, storytellers were able to walk people through the process of the story, rather than simply telling them the beginning and end factors. This meant that storytelling became an experience, both for the teller and the listener or reader. It was all thanks to story structure.

Although people weren't aware of what story structure actually was in the beginning, the idea of it emerged over time. It was identified as the structure of the story that was used to describe how certain characters within' the story dealt with problems and overcame them, as well as how they interacted with and communicated with other individuals from the story.

After identifying the concept of story structure and observing it from ancient storytelling experiences, people began using it as a general guideline for the process of building stories. Now, your story structure involves important information about the setting of your story, the people involved, the conflicts they experience, and how they overcome said conflicts. It is essentially every part of your story pulled together and planned out in a specific structure that helps you as the author understand what story you are trying to tell before and during the writing process.

Why You Need One

Having a story structure may seem pointless, especially if you already have the story in your head and you are simply attempting to get it out on paper. However, story structures are extremely valuable and can help you with the entire storytelling process. They are excellent for helping you identify how you are going to deliver the story to ensure that the reader receives the story effectively. This is more than simply providing the reader with information to help walk them from point a to point b. Instead, it is about giving them this relevant information in such a way that they are eager to know more and they stay actively engaged with the storytelling process.

When you design your story structure it helps you identify what your story sounds like to other people when they are reading it. It is important that you develop one before you start writing so that you have a strong execution plan going into the writing process. While you can simply write the story from your mind, this may result in you not emphasizing strong points enough, or otherwise diluting your story with information that takes away from it having a strong structure. Instead, you could plan your story out on paper first and essentially lay out the points that you will take your readers through within' the story. This way you can walk yourself through it and learn more about your story in advance. Doing this gives you the opportunity to identify any weak points and strengthen them, to ensure that your story makes sense and flows well, and to develop confidence in the idea that you have generated a strong enough plotline that your readers are going to stay actively engaged and enjoy the reading experience.

Now that you are more clear on what a story structure is and why it is so crucial to the writing process, it is time to explore the process of actually creating your own story structure so that you can embark on writing your own story. The following chapters will walk you through the step-by-step process of building your own story structure, as well as every technique you should know in order to have a strong structure that will leave your readers wanting more.

Chapter 2: The Essentials of Building a Structure

The first part of generating your own story structure is understanding the essentials. In this chapter, we are going to explore all of the basics that you should know when it comes to creating your own story structure. Throughout this chapter, you will be provided with tips and techniques to help you design the foundation of your structure. By the end, you should have a solid structure that will help you produce a phenomenal story.

9 Step Process

Most stories follow a typical nine-step process in order to generate their story structure. Some people prefer to alternate how the structure is designed, such as by introducing the climax in the first portion of the book. Still, they typically tend to break the book up into three main parts, or "acts" as they are called. This helps keep each part of the book focused on a certain subject that ultimately contributes to the overall story.

The following sections will introduce each step of the nine-step process and how they should be executed in order to produce a high-quality story structure. Please note that these are following the traditional method based on how many other stories have been structured throughout the ages. You may choose to alternate yours if you are more advanced, but if you are new to storytelling you will likely want to stick to and master this traditional structure before venturing into other structures. This will provide you with more practice towards developing a structure and using the purpose of the structure to your advantage. Once you are more skilled with structures then you can start to create alternative ones for your future stories because you will have a stronger idea about what makes them work and what doesn't.

Step One: First Act

The first step is to introduce the first act. This is the part of the story where you want to introduce the reader to your characters, the setting you have chosen, and anything that is at stake in the story. This is where they understand what is important and why. In the first act, you are given the opportunity to catch the attention of the reader and give them a reason to care about what story you are telling.

Example: You are writing a romance novel so you introduce the two lovers, as well as any other important characters to the reader. You will also take the time to provide insight as to where the book is taking place. This is where you can introduce the stakes as well, which essentially means you are telling the reader what is at stake and why it is important to the protagonist.

Step Two: The First Major Plot Point

The second step is to introduce the first major plot point to your reader. This should be defined by an event that takes place which forces the character to take action. You want this first major plot point to be considered the last scene in the first act so that readers are left wanting more. This is the finale of the first part of your book, so you want to leave it with some form of small cliffhanger. This both rewards the reader for reading by giving them some action to pay attention to, but also has them wondering what is going to come next as a result of the character's actions.

Example: The female character in your romance novel is walking home when an attacker tries to hurt her. The male character comes seemingly from nowhere and defends her honor, ensuring that she was protected and was not harmed by the attacker.

Step Three: First Half of Second Act

This is the part of the book where your character is coming back from the action they took at the end of the first act. Here you further explain what happened as a result of that plot point, as well as how your characters are dealing with it.

Example: As a result of him being the first to hit the attacker, despite him attempting to defend the female, the male role in your novel is being subjected to a criminal investigation. Because of this, he is trying to keep a low profile and avoid any further complications. The female is angry with the male for not calling the cops instead and allowing them to deal with it. She is upset that he has subjected himself to the criminal investigation through his actions, regardless of his reasoning.

Step Four: Second Major Plot Point

This is a plot point within' the story where the character who was attempting to regain their bearings from the first major plot point is forced back into action. Here, you want to work together with what said character has at stake to help the reader understand why they have been forced into action. Often the action is forced unto the character in the form of an ultimatum.

Example: Despite keeping a low profile for some time, the attacker returns and attempts to strike again. Only this time, he knows that the male is with the female and the attacker is attempting to force the male to act. He wants to have the male punished for attacking him, regardless of the fact that he was only attempting to protect her from the attacker. As a result, the male role is forced to decide between protecting her again or being faced with serious jail time. For the sake of these examples, let's say that he chooses to defend her honor once again.

Step Five: Second Half of Second Act

This is the part where all of the characters in the story begin to come into their own. Here, they are all grouping together to come against the antagonist. They are ensuring that the initial character is no longer left to take action on his or her own, but rather that they are supported by the other characters within' the story.

Example: This time, the female character is aware of what is going on and she is fighting to protect the male character. She is no longer angry with him for making the choice he made originally, and she is more willing to testify in his defense. They work together to get the attacker in trouble and to protect the male character through pleading that he was only practicing self-defense.

Step Six: Third Major Plot Point

This is where the protagonist's behavior appears to have led him or her to a place of defeat. In this part of the story, you want to introduce the idea that there may be no hope for this character and that they may be doomed because of the antagonistic forces. Here, they are beginning to feel as though they have hit rock bottom.

Example: Despite the female character testifying to the male character and fighting in his corner this time around, the court orders him guilty for assault. It appears that even though he was attempting to protect himself and the female character, no one is willing to see that. It seems there is no hope for him to avoid criminal charges altogether.

Step Seven: Third Act

In the third act, the protagonist is fighting against the antagonistic force as a last effort to take them down. Here they may not have total confidence that they can do it but they are not willing to give up just yet.

Example: The male character chooses to appeal the court ruling. Together, he and the female work to create a plan where they will prove that he is innocent and the attacker is the one who is truly guilty.

Step Eight: Climax

This is where there is a final face-off between the protagonist and antagonist. This is the deciding moment that is responsible for determining whether the story will end in favor of the antagonist, or in favor of the protagonist.

Example: The male character and the attacker face off in court. This is the part of the story that will determine whether the male is ruled guilty and is no longer welcome to appeal the charges, or whether the judge will see that he is actually innocent and it is the attacker who should be facing charges. For the sake of the example, we will say that it ends with the attacker being charged and the male being let off.

Step Nine: Resolution

This is where any loose ends from the story. It will also give insight to how the characters react to the climax and where they end up afterward. This is the wind down where readers are given the opportunity to know "what's next" and is required to avoid you from ending your book in a cliff-hanger.

Example: The female character is ecstatic that the male character is let free and they decide that they never want to risk facing a life without the other so they choose to get married.

As you can see, developing a strong story structure is important. Hopefully, through the use of the examples, you were able to understand how the structure lent a hand towards generating suspense and giving the reader a reason to keep reading. Because of how the story was structured and when certain pieces of information were revealed, the individual reading the story once it was complete would be engaged and would thus stay committed to reading the entire story so that they could discover how it ended.

It is important that you pay attention to the book in three sections as outlined above, as well as that you have a major plot point in each part. Dividing your story into three sections ensures that each part focuses on a particular element of the story and avoids you from going back and forth or otherwise introducing elements that are later forgotten about because you are not clear and focused on what you are writing. Having a major plot point in each section ensures that each section is rich and your reader is engaged the entire time. This is ultimately the structure you need in order to draw your reader forward and keep them moving through the story until they reach the end.

Chapter 3: Developing Your Story

Now that you are aware of what it takes to design a strong story structure, you may be wondering how you can develop a story that will fit with the structure! If you already have a general idea, then you can use the information from this section to help you strengthen that idea and ensure that all areas of your story are considered before them being structured and then written. If you have no idea as to what your story is going to be yet, use this chapter to help you identify a story and develop it so that it provides you with plenty of material to write your book about.

Study Existing Plots

When you are working towards developing your story one of the best ways to go about it is to read. Reading other people's stories gives you the opportunity to see what worked and what didn't, and it also provides you with inspiration to enrich your own story. While you don't want to be plagiarizing or stealing stories from other people, getting inspiration to enrich your own and strengthen the plot is always a great idea. This ensures that you are going to have a really strong story that provides enough material to engage your audience and keep them captive for the duration of the book.

When you are studying other people's stories you want to do more than just read them. You want to pay attention to who the characters are, how they develop throughout the novel, how the events take place including when and where, and all locations that the story takes place in. You should also identify the sequence that the locations are used in. Knowing more about these primary areas of the story allows you to get an idea of how books are written and what authors do in order to develop their own storyline. You can see the techniques in action and understand how they contribute to the overall experience being delivered in the story.

Draft Up Your Plot

When you are designing your plot there are some strategies you can use to see your plot come together without writing out the entire story first. The best way to do this is through drafting up your plot. You can do this by writing a paragraph or two from each ideal chapter and then read them in order. While it will obviously be missing many details, doing this will give you an idea of how the plot points flow together and if they are strong enough to give you plenty of writing material to work with.

Using a plotting strategy like this gives you the opportunity to look at your plot as a whole and make sure that it works effectively in the story you are writing. This helps you see what areas of the plot are rich and which aren't. You can also finalize the main plot sequencing and points before starting the writing process so that you are certain that it is in the order that you want and that it all works well together. This essentially gives you a birds-eye view of what your structure is and lets you know whether or not it works.

Create a Timeline

A great way to build your story is to create a timeline. This timeline should include all of the major plot points in chronological order. Seeing these together helps you identify how each one builds into the next one and makes sure that they work well together. If anything is missing or you feel there is a plot point that does not fit well in the overall story, then you can use this as an opportunity to eliminate it.

Similar to drafting your plot, creating a timeline allows you to take a birds-eye view at the work you have created and determine whether or not it works. The more you pay attention to the structure of your story from different elements now, the more you can be certain that it will work and produce a strong story in the long run.

Plan Character Development Along the Plot Line

After you have generated your plot draft and your timeline, take your characters into consideration. Pay attention to how you want them to develop along the storyline. It is natural for characters to change throughout stories, and even necessary in order for the story to progress. A great way to plan their development is to plan it alongside the story development. How is the development of the story going to contribute to the growth of the character? Consider this while you are deciding how your character will develop along the way.

Change the 5 "W's

A great way to ensure that you have developed the story strong enough is to check that you have changed the five w's along the way. The who, what, when, where, and why of the story should all develop or completely change along the progression of your story. In real life, these change from moment to moment and

169

day to day. If you want your story to be realistic and relatable, you need to ensure that they are changed in your story as well.

If you want to take your story from good to great, these answers should not be simple and direct. Each one should have a series of answers that guide the element from the start of the book to the end. They should change in a way that convinces the reader that the change was natural and realistic, and helps the character feel as though it is a true story being told. Think back to your own day, for example you may have woken up in your home and now you are sitting in a coffee shop reading this book. You may have woken in a bad mood and now you are in a better one, or vice versa. The reasons as to why your mood change are also important to the story of your day. Who was involved in your day and what helped you pass the day by will have also changed from moment to moment. Just like your day naturally progressed as a story of its own, you need your story to progress in the same way. This ensures that your book goes in-depth enough to make it convincing to your reader. If any of the five w's are not developed enough, look for opportunities to strengthen them so that your story will be rich and full of realistic details.

Design a Story Board

Creating a storyboard is another great way to look at the structure of your story. A great way to create the storyboard is to write each major plot point and important element on a cue card or post it so that they can easily be moved around to create the final story map. This gives you a great opportunity to see how each event works together and organize them effortlessly without having to scratch out things and replace them everywhere.

Consider Subplots

Creating subplots that fit in seamlessly with your overall story is a great way to enrich the story experience and add more depth to it while also encouraging reader engagement. Subplots are essentially the "what else" part of the story. For example, if you are writing a book about the main character who is seeking justice, consider including elements of why this justice is so important for this character. Perhaps they want the criminal incarcerated because he or she deserves to be, but it may also be because the protagonist has allowed others to walk all over him for too long and he is ready to stand up for himself. Therefore, getting justice is both about having justice served *and* about building the confidence to actually fight for what is right.

Subplots are an incredible story developing strategy that can help you create a story that is much richer in context. You can include as many or as few subplots as you want, but make sure that each one makes sense to the overall story itself. They should work together with the main plot, rather than going against it or straying away from it completely.

Incorporate Driven Elements

All of the best stories incorporate one specific element that enables the story to be so great. That is the element of change. In order to create change, there are two very specific things you need. Character-driven and action-driven elements to your story. These elements are two things that can help incorporate change into your story in such a way that yours fosters all of the greatness that all of the other best titles do.

The reason why change is so powerful in a story is that that is what drives the story forward. People are curious to know about how characters change and grow throughout the course of the story every bit as much as they are interested in learning about how the story develops itself. People do not want to read a story about static characters who do the same thing every day and nothing changes. That would be extremely boring and would lead to them closing the book and turning away from it entirely. Think about it, would you read a book like that? Likewise, people are not interested in a book that has minimal change, or where the change only occurs on one very specific thing. Instead, people want to see the entire story change. They want to see the characters grow, they want to see the circumstances evolve, and they want to see the protagonist, and even the antagonist, end up somewhere completely different from where they were when the story changed. Incorporating as much natural and realistic change as possible helps drive your story forward and keep it both interesting and engaging.

As previously mentioned, there are two different types of change you can use to drive your story forward: character-driven change, and action-driven change. Both of these elements should be included in your own story if you want a diverse and realistic story that will help keep your readers engaged and reading your book all the way until the last page.

Character-driven change is used by showing the stakes the character has. For example, their child, their family, their significant other, their career. By incorporating these stakes and giving the reader insight as to why they are so important to the character, you can use them as an opportunity to drive the story forward. The most important thing to understand is that without character-driven change, there is no story. Character-driven change is essentially the answer to "why" your character is doing anything that takes place in the story. This explains why they will do almost anything, even stuff that seems highly irrational or nonsensical, in various situations. "Because my child is sick" or, "because I could lose my job" for example, would be the stakes and therefore would answer "why" the character is so invested in something. By creating this type of explanation and therefore emotional attachment from the reader to the character, and furthermore the character's stakes, you can make virtually every part of the story that much more engaging and interesting for your reader. Without character-driven change, your readers are not given an opportunity to understand why they need to care about the events taking place in your book.

Action-driven change is an entirely different form of change. This is the change whereby specific actions happen that cause the story to drive forward. High-speed chases, break-ins, getting arrested, being put on the chopping block at work, the spouse falling in love with someone else, the kid getting into trouble, all of these would constitute as action-drive changes. For the most part, these are actions that are taking place that cannot be stopped or influenced by your protagonist. Instead, the protagonist must find a way to respond and react to these actions.

When you use character-driven change effectively, action-driven change becomes that much more intriguing and engaging for your reader. Because they understand the stakes and have developed an emotional attachment to your characters, they are much more concerned with the action, as well as the outcome. It is important that you use a balanced amount of both types of changes in your story. This will help you round out your story and keep it moving forward without being too heavily charged in one direction or another. Furthermore, you want to make sure that you don't go overboard on the change. While it does drive the story forward, you want to make sure that you use it in a very realistic and natural manner. This helps the reader relate to the story and believe it, instead of feeling as though it is completely unlikely and therefore it is not relatable. If a reader cannot relate to a story in one way or another, they are not going to continue reading it because it will be too unbelievable for them.

Question Yourself

When you are in the process of developing your story, make sure you question yourself a lot along the way. The more you question yourself, your intentions, the story and the plot line, the more you can develop it. Questioning it ultimately gives you the opportunity to see where any loopholes may lie, if any part of the plot is weak, or if there is any reason that you should need to develop part of the story more. It also helps you identify where there may be too much action or development going on so that you can scale it back. If you are not taking the time to question yourself and your story structure, you may be missing important things that could take away from the value of your story altogether.

Some great questions to ask yourself include ones such as:

- Why has the character changed, how did the change happen, and what was the purpose of this change?

- How much has the character changed since the beginning of the story?

- Is the change natural and believable?

- What has each plot point taught the characters, thus teaching them about the story's primary situation or conflict?

- Can you identify some core themes within' the story? Are there too many or too few core themes taking place?

- Is the story believable? Does it flow naturally?

- Does the story move forward effectively, or is it too slow?

Asking yourself these questions will help ensure that each part of your story structure is strong and that it will help you produce a believable, relatable, and enjoyable story that is interesting and engaging. If you find that your answer is "no" or "I don't know" to any of the questions above, take the time to further explore that question and find ways that you can strengthen the story structure itself.

Get Feedback

Finally, it is important that you take the time to get feedback on your story structure. As with most things, having someone else take a look and give you some insight as to where the strengths and weaknesses lie and if any adaptations or alterations should be made means that nothing will be missed. This is the best way to make sure that you have a strong structure going into your story that will both serve you and serve your readers by giving you enough material and answers to generate an interesting an engaging story.

If you do not personally know someone who can provide you with feedback, there are many online platforms and forums that you can turn to where you can find someone to help you with looking over the structure. Furthermore, you can also look to find someone from your ideal target audience and have them look over the structure for you. Regardless of who you get to help you with the structure, do your best to make sure it is someone who is either in or thoroughly understands your target audience, and ideally someone with some experience in story structure. Having someone who intimately knows you are trying to reach and what you are trying to say can help significantly as it ensures that any feedback or critique they provide you with is accurate and helpful. Those who are unclear on the audience you are trying to reach or who have zero understanding of story structure or what is required in order to make a good book may not be able to provide you with information that will help you improve your structure. In fact, they may even have you questioning parts that you should not need to question. It is important that the person you choose to work with understands your needs.

Chapter 4: Creating Suspense

Regardless of what genre you are writing for, you need to be skilled in creating suspense for your story. Suspense is the element that keeps readers wondering what is coming next and how events are going to unfold. When used properly, suspense can be what draws one plot point to the next. If you want to create a compelling and convincing fiction novel that encourages readers to continue reading, you are going to need to master the art of creating suspense. The next ten tips are about how you can begin creating suspense in your own novel to keep your readers wanting more.

Understand Your Genre

Before you begin creating suspense, it is important that you understand the genre you are writing in. Each genre uses suspense differently to draw characters forward and keep readers coming back. If you want to do your book justice, you need to practice using suspense for your unique genre.

Let's take a look at three different types of novels and where the suspense would come into play for each type.

Mystery: A horror or major event takes place in the first chapter and the rest of the book is spent figuring out why the event occurred and who was responsible for it. For example, the protagonist's spouse was killed in the first chapter and the rest of the book is spent uncovering who was responsible.

Romance: You build up to the point where the two lovers finally get together. The climax, or the two getting together, officially takes place later in the book, usually within' the last couple of chapters. For example, two lovers know they're meant to be together but the timing never seems right. One is always dating someone else when the other is available for the relationship to work. As a result, they are never able to get together until the end when they finally make it work.

Suspense: The knowledge of an impending horror is upon the characters in the novel and they spend the entire time trying to avoid it until they can no longer keep it from happening. For example, someone knows they are going to jail for embezzlement but doesn't know when. This character knows that he has been tracked and that the FBI is well aware of what has been going on. He does not know when he will be taken down, but it will happen.

Provide Adequate Viewpoints

When it comes to developing a strong case of suspense in your novel, you need to give the reader adequate knowledge. This comes from providing them with different viewpoints. Through this, you can give them insight to the protagonist's side of things, and the antagonist's side of things. The best way to get a lot of suspense building in your book is by giving your reader insight as to what is going to happen before the protagonist knows. This gives the writer the opportunity to increase the emotional attachment to the protagonist and the stakes. The reader is drawn along an experience where they know what is yet to come but they have to watch the protagonist find out and learn the consequences of certain actions. The tension that builds on the reader because of what they know that the protagonist doesn't know is similar to someone who has a secret they're not allowed to tell. It engages the reader and makes them want to know more and to understand where the book will end up.

Put Time on Your Side

Time is an incredible tool when it comes to writing a book with suspense. You want to use time on your side so that you can increase the amount of suspense in the novel. Time gives you the opportunity to make the reader feel as though the protagonist is working against the clock. Everything they are doing should have some form of time constraint on it. Ideally, it should appear as though the clock is working in favor of the antagonist or antagonistic force to keep the suspense strong. For example, if you were writing a mystery novel about a murder that took place, it should seem as though the protagonist doesn't have enough time to find the murderer. Perhaps there is some jurisdiction law that states that if the person is not found within' a set amount of time the charges won't be as strong, or the murderer has been leaving clues that they have left town and it gets harder and harder to find who they are. Several dead end leads are exhausted before the protagonist finally discovers who the murderer was in the end. Putting time on your side lets you build suspense by creating the illusion that something won't happen, even though it needs to.

Keep The Stakes High

The stakes that you use in a story should be high enough to justify a high amount of suspense. The higher the stakes the more pressing the need to protect them is, both in the mind of the character and the reader. While you don't need to choose devastating stakes that are excessively high, picking ones that someone would actually be desperate to protect will ensure that your reader understands why the protagonist is so passionate about protecting their stakes. Some examples would include an executive who is facing being exposed for shady business dealings, therefore costing them their job and their reputation and making them unlikeable for other employers. Or, perhaps a male is in love with a female in a romance novel, but he grows tired of waiting for her to make up her mind so he pursues a relationship with someone else. She realizes she wants him more than anything but must figure out a way to tell him, and fast, before he marries the other person or realizes that he does not want to be with her altogether. Alternatively, you may choose to write a story about someone with a powerful societal position being murdered and they must find out who did it before they strike another powerful member of society. By keeping the stakes high but reasonable, you make it very clear as to why your reader needs to be so concerned with what is taking place in the book. The stronger your stakes are, the more your reader will be passionate alongside your character to ensure that they are not lost.

Don't Be Afraid to Apply Pressure

Pressure is a great way to add suspense to any novel. The odds should be stacked well against your character and it should take a great amount of effort and energy for them to tip the odds in their favor and save the day. The more the odds are stacked against them, the higher the pressure is and therefore the more you can draw the reader to wondering if they will ever be able to beat the odds. When they finally do, the reader and character alike will feel a great deal of relief from the experience.

When you are writing about creating pressure, make sure that you never lead your protagonist right to the breaking point. They should bend and cripple under pressure, but they should never stop pushing. You should ensure that they are always pushed *almost* too far so that they have *just* enough amount of energy to push back and it is at that time that they finally beat the antagonistic force and experience success in their heroic attempts.

Make Use of Dilemmas

Dilemmas are a great way to increase suspense in a story and have your reader highly engaged. Dilemmas present a "this or that" action for the character. They should be forced into action, and make sure that the pressure is on for it to happen fast. When dilemmas are being thrown towards your character it is important to make sure that they are being thrown by the antagonist most often. This should present the idea that the protagonist cannot win in the situation. For example, for them to save one character another must die, they can either lose their family and save their job or lose their job and save their family, or even indulging in alcohol after swearing to sobriety at some point within' the novel.

When you are presenting dilemmas, make sure that the antagonist always crosses the line. Because they are the villain, they shouldn't even think twice about going across it. However, the protagonist should always be forced with their morals and values. Should they do one, or the other? Which will be the less of two evils? Is there a way that they can make the best of both horrible situations? True to heroic nature, they should be struggling to find the answer to the dilemma.

One great reason why dilemmas work is because you can apply pressure and time constraints so that the protagonist is forced to make a decision fast, which puts pressure on him and gets the reader worried about what is going to happen. Using these three strategies together is a great way to build suspense throughout your book.

Complicate Things

You don't need to restrict to just presenting your protagonist with one or even two conflicts at any given time. Instead, feel free to pile on the complications every now and again. The more complicated things get, the more difficult it will be for them to come up with the solution and make the right choice. At times, it should feel like the protagonist is trying to juggle several balls at once and he is just barely keeping them from dropping every time. This is a great time to push the protagonist almost to the point of breaking before bringing them back in for a final and much awaited victory.

Avoid Becoming Predictable

When your book runs too smoothly, it becomes predictable. It also becomes uninteresting and the readers struggle to relate to it. Life is not about being smooth and predictable. Most often we are all living in a hot mess where we are balancing many different things and trying to stay afloat along the way. If you want to write a great book, it should be similar to this. Throw random curveballs in, take a spin somewhere where one wasn't expected, and have your reader surprised at some of the elements that are being tossed in, and when. When it comes to writing, don't let the hero rely on the idea that everything will go in their favor. In fact, almost nothing should. This way when it finally does, it will come as a surprise. Furthermore, your antagonist shouldn't go with everything going in their way, either. Let both of them face challenges, twists and turns along the way. The more they are affected by curveballs and unexpected experiences, the more realistic the story will be. Make the protagonist slip up and result in an almost-victory instead of a true victory, and let the antagonist fail at the most inconvenient of times for them. This keeps your readers on their toes and unsure about what is going to happen, when.

Develop Your Villain

Your villain is the antagonistic force in your book, and they need to be developed really well. Your reader should be mentally pushing against the villain, and rooting for the hero. As a result, you need to have a really well developed villain that has the reader truly believing and feeling as though they are a nasty force to be reckoned with.

Make sure that you use the right villain for your novel genre, as well. In a mystery, for example, it should not be clear as to who the villain is until the end. With a romance novel on the other hand, the villain might be time itself, or the person coming between the two lovers and keeping them apart. Alternatively, in a suspense novel the villain should be highly visible at all times and people should ultimately just be wondering when they will finally strike. The more you understand what type of villain is appropriate for your unique genre, the easier it will be to create one that is believable and extremely well developed.

When you develop your antagonist, make sure that you are very specific on who they are and what makes them tick. You want this character to be so developed that your reader feels as though they personally know them. Furthermore, your antagonist should change throughout the story, which is easiest to prove if your reader knows who they are from how you've written about them.

Develop Your Hero

In addition to developing your villain, you need to develop your hero. This is the one that finally defeats the antagonistic force and creates the victory of the story. The best way to create a strong hero is to really build on the character and give the reader plenty of reasons to love them. This is the character your reader is going to follow throughout the story. This is who they will be rooting for, worrying for, and curious about. They want to know everything they can about this character, and they have mentally prepared themselves to be on their side emotionally. Therefore, you need to use this character to not only build an emotional attachment between your reader and your protagonist, but also to use that attachment to manipulate the emotions of your reader. The protagonist is the character that you are going to leverage in order to get your reader nervous, curious, excited, happy, sad, angry, and any other emotion you want them to engage in throughout the experience. The best way to do that is to have a well-developed character that your reader can truly feel as though they have befriended.

Chapter 5: Additional Story Structure Tips

In addition to tips on basic story structure, developing a strong story, and how to create suspense, there are many other great tips that can help you when it comes to story structures. Now that you have the three important elements down, you can explore additional tips that will take you further into the realm of pro writer and help you generate a story that is going to be fantastic. The following tips are provided from real authors who have experience in writing their own high quality fiction materials. By following these tips, you can ensure that you don't only have a great story structure, but a phenomenal one.

Research Different Story Structures

Although there is a basic system that virtually all structures follow, it is important to understand that there are many modifications and alterations made to this structure in true writing. After all, if every story followed the basic structure down to the last detail then there would be no point in reading. We would be able to read the first chapter and know exactly how a book was going to turn out. By making modifications to the structure and playing it around in different ways, writers have the ability to stick to a structure that works while also providing a script that is unique, unpredictable, and engaging for readers.

Armed with this knowledge, you can prepare yourself to start researching many different story structures. The best way is to read other people's novels and do your best to identify the structure within' them. As you are reading, write down the major plot points and other key details that come into play with these plot points. Doing this will help you identify a series of structures that are used to create incredible novels, and how the writers spun them to work for the story. Do this several times over and pay attention to patterns that arise. Then, choose the structure you like most and make it work for your novel!

Stick to Structures that Are Traditional for Your Genre

For the best results, it is important that you stick to structures that are traditional to your genre. Although this may sound like a surefire way to create a story that sounds like every other story in the genre, it actually isn't. You will learn more about why in a moment. In the meantime, it is important that you understand why it is a good idea to stick to these traditional structures.

Each structure is designed to create a different effect for the story. Some build suspense, some build mystery, and some build both. Depending on what genre you are writing for, you are going to want to go for a structure that provides you with the right elements of virtually everything. These are going to be elements of suspense, story building opportunities, character development opportunities, and more. Each genre tends to be told in a unique way because it achieves a specific result. Therefore, each structure that is unique to each genre is built to help achieve that specific result. For example, you wouldn't want to use a suspense structure for a mystery novel because you would thus be identifying the perpetrator immediately. Likewise, you wouldn't want to use a mystery structure in a suspense novel because it would destroy the element of suspense by not giving enough information to the reader.

It is important that you do not reinvent the wheel, but rather you explore the different styles of wheels that exist for your market. Furthermore, just because you are limited to only using structures that are traditional for your genre does not mean that there is only one single structure you can follow. Each genre has its own selection of structures that will and won't work. The best way to identify which one you want to use is to read them, as described in the previous section, and pay attention to each type of structure you come across. As you do, identify which one would work best for your unique story and enlist that as your structure of choice.

Structure the Novel to Your Central Theme

As you are designing the structure for your novel, make sure that you are conforming the structure to fit the central theme of your novel and not the other way around. You never want to be derailing or detracting from the story as an attempt to stick to your structure. Remember, a structure is supposed to be a guideline that gets you to where you need to go. You do not have to follow it down to every last detail in order for your story to be a good one. Instead, you want to pay attention to the story structure and write your novel with that structure in mind.

Stories that are written to strictly to the guidelines set out in the structure end up sounding very forced and uncomfortable. Readers will often lose engagement quickly because the story becomes predictable and unnatural. They cannot relate to the story so they do not want to read it any longer. Ultimately, it takes away from the reader's experiences and kills the chance of your novel being greater.

To elaborate on how the structure *should* be used, we will explore how exactly you can enforce its guidelines. One of the biggest things you want to pay attention to, and use your structure for, is to ensure that your book stays focused on the central theme. If your novel strays too far away from the central theme at any given point, it may take away from the story overall. You never want to over share or get off track on a topic that does not contribute to the central theme or purpose of your novel. This is where your story structure comes in handy. Having a structure that can help keep you on track is highly valuable as it ensures that you do not derail your story and end up with a novel about love that gets too off track and ends up being about one person's career, or something else. Essentially you want to employ your story structure as a guide to keep you on track and to build a strong story, but you do not want to follow it so closely that you snuff out the quality of your story and produce something generic and predictable.

Modify the Template to Suit Your Plot

To expand further on the previous tip, it is important to work on modifying your template to suit your plot. Although you do not want to create an entirely new structure for your novel, or take one from the wrong genre, this does not mean that you cannot modify the template. For example, if you would prefer a certain plot point to happen sooner rather than later, or vice versa, you certainly have creative freedom to make this decision. Remember, you are a storyteller and your story is your work of art. Just because there are certain methods to use doesn't mean you can't get creative. For example, paint brushes are what you are *supposed* to paint with, but many choose to paint with sponges or even rags instead. Some even use a different material altogether, and yet the art is still incredible beautiful. In fact, it may be even more beautiful because of the unique method used. In this analogy, a different approach was used but the same bare basic structure was used: a tool was used to pick up paint and apply it to a canvas. You can easily modify certain parts of that, such as by changing your tools or picking a unique canvas, but at the very root is the same structure. The same goes for writing.

Just because authors before you have always used a specific template doesn't mean you cannot modify that template to suit your story. If you find that certain elements would serve better at a different area in the story, you are always welcome to do that. The best thing you can do as a writer is exercise your creative freedom. When you let loose from expectations and open yourself up to generate phenomenal content, inevitably you generate phenomenal content. As long as you stick to the bare bones basics with your structure, you are going to end up with a great story. If on the off chance you don't, it is a great opportunity to further research the structure and understand where you went wrong and how you could create a better story and structure in the future.

Create the Structure First, Modify it Later

It is always a good idea to begin your story with a strong structure. That being said, you should seek to create the structure before you begin writing. Having your structure created first and then creating a story around that structure helps ensure that you are staying on track with the basics. However, that does not mean that you are restricted to only writing to that specific structure.

As writers carry along the process of writing, they often find that it takes them down a natural path and therefore certain elements of their original structure no longer serve the story as powerfully as they could. The best thing to do in this circumstances is to reevaluate the structure and modify it so that it better suits the story in the direction that you have taken it. When you do this, you open yourself up to the opportunity of creating something much more powerful than you originally set out to do.

Creating a story is not always as straightforward as it seems. In many cases you will go into it with a very specific idea of what you want the story to be like and as a result of your writing process you discover that it actually works for reasons other than you thought so it naturally evolves away from your initial intentions. The best thing you can do in these circumstances is honor that natural evolution in your story and work with it. If you try and go against it in order to stick to your original structure you may end up creating a strange and unnatural twist backward, or it will otherwise not flow well. In order to give yourself creative freedom while also holding on to some sense of direction, the best thing to do is to start with a structure and modify it if your story evolves away from the initial structure you laid out for it. This will keep you on track while also giving you the potential to create an incredible story.

Hide the Structure in Your Writing

When it comes to the writing process, you want to ensure that you are hiding the structure within' your writing. It should not be painfully obvious what structure you have used. If it is, then your story will become predictable and people will lose interest. Virtually every story structure has been used several times over. This means that people will have a pretty easy ability to link your strategies together and determine what the novel will end like regardless of whether or not they have read it. They will also likely discover what major plot points are going to occur well before they ever happen. When the book becomes this predictable, it also becomes highly uninteresting.

A great writer knows how to hide the structure within' the story. Make things happen sooner or later than expected, twist away from the structure here and there to blend it in, and do your best to avoid going very clearly from point one to point two. You want your readers to question what is happening and be surprised along the way. Give them the idea that they have already arrived at the major plot point with one activity and then blow them out of the water with something much bigger. Keep the element of surprise active and use it as your weapon to bury the structure. The less obvious your structure is, the more unpredictable your story becomes and therefore the more power you have as the author to keep your reader engaged and have them wanting to learn more about what you have yet to tell them.

Keep Your Structure Organized and Handy

For a practical writing tip in regards to your structure, it is important that you keep it organized and that it is available at all times when you are writing. Your structure will prove to be a highly valuable tool when it comes to producing your novel. Being able to refer back to it at different points and identify where you are at will help you know where to go with your story, as well as help you stay focused on the central theme and overall purpose of your book.

A great way to keep your structure handy and useful during the writing process is to have it written down somewhere, such as on cue cards, and nearby whenever you are writing. This way you can identify where you have already been on the structure and where you have yet to go. It will also provide you with the ability to refer back to it regularly, as well as effortlessly revise it as needed. The reason why you might want to make your "final" structure on cue cards is because if you choose to modify it along the way you can easily do it without having to completely start over or rewrite it. This makes it effortless for you to modify it as needed and keep the parts you want.

Experiment

There is nothing more valuable than hands-on practice when it comes to any hobby, and this fact is not lost on writing. If you are looking for an opportunity to create an incredible book, take any chance you have to experiment. There are many ways that you can experiment when it comes to writing, and each can help you increase your understanding of story structures and how they work into the overall book, as well as how you can use your unique writing style to make the most of your story structure.

One great method is to take note of a few different story structures that will work effectively for the genre you are writing in and then draft your story out based on these. This means that you want to write a few paragraphs on each part of the structure and then read them together. It will give you the opportunity to see how your story would work together and if you have generated a strong enough story structure for your book. Another method is to practice writing short stories with different structures in a smaller way. While you won't be able to pack as much into the story as you would with a novel, it will give you a better idea of how your novel would sound with each unique structure in place.

Experimentation is the best way to practice writing and get an idea for what you like and what you don't like. If you are serious about it and you have time, practicing writing each novel with different structures and employing different strategies is a great way to see each structure in action and get a feel for how it works for your books. You can identify how the structure serves your story and where it might be weak, as well as how you can embed the structure within' the story using unique writing strategies to hide it from plain sight. This is a great way to practice writing overall and increase your skill if you are interested and have the time to invest.

Take Notes

Finally, a great method to use when it comes to learning and growing as a writer or as virtually anything is to take notes. When you are reading other books, take notes on what you like and don't like about the book, particularly when it comes to the structure of the book. When you are writing your own books, pay attention to where you have struggled and where you are succeeding. On the points where you a struggling, explore ways that you could make it easier. When it comes to each unique structure, write down how it serves your story and any thoughts you might have about how it could be better next time, or when you go through the editing process.

Taking notes allows you to review what you have already thought and felt about certain experiences with your story and its structure and gives you something easy and finite to look back on. When you take notes it means that you are not going to forget about or lose your thoughts in the process. This means that you can hold onto them and make the necessary changes without having to attempt to remember what it was that you wanted to do in the first place.

There are many great strategies you can use to strengthen your story structure immediately, as well as to help you increase your skills and become a better story writer through your structure over time. The more you emphasize on learning this skill now, the greater you will be at is as you go on. Remember that a strong structure can truly make or break a story. A bad structure equals a bad story, a good one equals a good story and a great structure will return you a great story. If you want to be great, you have to practice being great from the start. Over time and with practice you will graduate from being great to being

phenomenal!

Conclusion

Thank you for reading *"Story Structure: Step-by-Step | Essential Story Building, Story Development and Suspense Writing Tricks Any Writer Can Learn"*. This book was designed to assist you in learning everything you need to know about story structures, including how you can make an incredible one.

I hope this book was able to elaborate on the concept of story structures, including what they are and why they are important. I also hope that you were able to learn plenty about how you can create your own story structure, develop your story, create suspense, and ultimately strengthen the structure of your story in order to create a phenomenal book.

The next step is to build your story structure and use it alongside the creation of your new book. Take your time and follow the steps within' this book to ensure that you have a strong structure that will serve you in the process of creating your book. Remember, as you go about the writing process you will want to check back to your structure to ensure that you are sticking to your original plan. However, if you find that your structure is no longer serving the overall creation of your story, you can always modify your structure for stronger impact. Sometimes the writing process can alter our plans and take us down a separate natural path. If this happens, ensure that you use the structure to support your story and the other way around.

Thank you!

More by Sandy Marsh

Discover all books from the Writing Best Seller Series by Sandy Marsh at:

bit.ly/sandy-marsh

Book 1: *How to Write a Novel*

Book 2: *Outlining*

Book 3: *Story Structure*

Book 4: *Plotting*

Book 5: *Character Development*

Book 6: *How to Write a Screenplay*

Themed book bundles available at discounted prices:

bit.ly/sandy-marsh